PRAISE FOR *SEEK TO BE WISE*

"I had the privilege of working with Chess for over 30 years! In all those years, the characteristic I most admired in him was his wisdom. I always referred to him as the 'Wise Old Owl' of our company. His wisdom and leadership helped guide us through the toughest of times. In this book, Chess distills this timeless wisdom into down-to-earth principles that everyone can benefit from."

—JOHN ADDISON, CEO & PRESIDENT,
ADDISON LEADERSHIP GROUP, INC.,
FORMER CO-CEO, PRIMERICA

"I've always been fascinated by the earliest days and years of life—the way children absorb the world around them like sponges. Physical changes aside, they mature, develop and grow most dramatically by learning from the small world around them. Every day they discover deep, lasting truths about themselves, the world, and their place in it. Over time and especially into adulthood, as our world expands, our curiosity, sadly, tends to fade.

Chess Britt has therefore hit a bull's eye on one of the most vital aspects of personal success: the lifelong search for wisdom. While the most important lessons are always closest to home, the journey never stops."

—JOSH ELLIS, EDITOR-IN-CHIEF,
SUCCESS MAGAZINE

"In *Seek to Be Wise,* Britt gives away the secret to a life well lived: above all else, 'Seek to be wise!' This book is filled with stories illustrating timeless bits of wisdom he has acquired along his life's path. In a humble, yet insightful way, Britt shares 31 maxims—timeless truths—he picked up from family, friends, co-workers, and popular culture. This is not a book you'll want to read and put on a shelf; this is a book you'll want to refer to again and again."

—DR. BARY FLEET, LIFE COACH,
EDUCATOR, SPEAKER, AND AUTHOR OF
THE BEST-SELLING BOOK, *MOVE INTO YOUR
MAGNIFICENCE: 101 INVITATIONS TO
A LIFE OF PASSION AND JOY*

Finding Extraordinary Wisdom
IN EVERYDAY LIFE

SEEK
TO BE
WISE

CHESS BRITT

GREENLEAF
BOOK GROUP PRESS

Published by Greenleaf Book Group Press
Austin, Texas
www.gbgpress.com

Distributed by Greenleaf Book Group

For ordering information or special discounts for bulk purchases, please contact Greenleaf Book Group at PO Box 91869, Austin, TX 78709, 512.891.6100.

Design and composition by Greenleaf Book and Rachael Brandenburg
Cover design by Greenleaf Book Group Rachael Brandenburg
Cover image: ©istock/uuoott

Publisher's Cataloging-in-Publication data is available.

Print ISBN: 978-1-62634-721-2

eBook ISBN: 978-1-62634-722-9

Part of the Tree Neutral® program, which offsets the number of trees consumed in the production and printing of this book by taking proactive steps, such as planting trees in direct proportion to the number of trees used: www.treeneutral.com

TreeNeutral

Printed in the United States of America on acid-free paper

20 21 22 23 24 25   10 9 8 7 6 5 4 3 2 1

First Edition

In memory of Dad.
In honor of Mom.
The pillars of my life.

And to Grayson. A little wisdom from "Pops."

"Wisdom is not a product of schooling, but of the lifelong attempt to acquire it."

—*Albert Einstein*

CONTENTS

ACKNOWLEDGMENTS

LIFE BLESSED ME WITH WONDERFUL parents—Barbara and Gene Britt. You are the pillars of my life. Any success I have, I owe it all to you.

Trisha, Chess, and Matt—you are the greatest blessings in my life. Trisha, I love you and appreciate all you do. You have loved me and shared your life with me for over forty years, and there is no one I would rather spend my life with. I look forward to our future. I am confident the best is yet to come. Chess and Matt—you are the world to me. I am proud to be your dad. I give thanks every day for you, and pray God will be with you.

This book would have never happened if it had not been for Monica Lewis. Your help and encouragement in the early stages are the reasons it kept moving forward. I am grateful for your time and talent. You're the best!

To Danny Woodard—I have always valued your good judgment and honesty. Your thoughts on the early manuscript encouraged me to double down on my efforts.

To John Addison—your valuable input on the early manuscript helped me see the next steps. Thanks for that input and your leadership. But most of all thank, you for your friendship. We have shared a lot of good times, and I am certain there are many more to come.

Thanks to Larry Weidel for recommending that I contact Greenleaf Book Group. The team at Greenleaf have been remarkable. Sally Garland—your input and wise coaching brought clarity to the message. Thank you, also, Aaron Teel and Elizabeth Chenette for your outstanding work.

I will be forever grateful to all of my family, friends, and acquaintances who shared their lives with me. They inspired and guided me in my search for wisdom.

To Rick Mathis—who has been my best friend since the second grade. I am thankful that you encouraged me to come to work at Primerica. That decision changed my life.

To my teammates at Primerica, the greatest group of men and women in North America—you have blessed me with your leadership and inspiration. There is no better place for a kid from Grayson, Georgia, to have started his career. It was an extraordinary thirty-six years. Glenn Williams—you have done an incredible job as CEO. I appreciate your leadership and the opportunity to have worked with you. Your hard work, dedication, and character are remarkable. Andy Young, and Bobby and Red Buission—your team-first approach to business, leadership, and life make you the teammates I aspired to be. Bobby—thanks for meeting with me and sharing your chapter three. Your words planted the seed that maybe I had something to share. Andy— you have a way of putting things in perspective and can see bull crap sooner and clearer than anyone I have known. When I proofread a chapter, I used W*hat would Andy think?* as a filter. I hope I hit the mark.

Most of all, I am grateful to you, the reader, for using your valuable time to read my message. It is my honor to share my thoughts with you. My prayer is that it was time well spent.

Prologue

THE SIMPLE IS EXTRAORDINARY

WISDOM IS CALLING: WHY NOT answer the call?

Whatever you seek in life, wisdom will lead you in the right direction.

Some people are seeking spiritual success; others want personal success. Maybe you are seeking financial or business success. Whatever you are after, allowing wisdom to guide your search will make all the difference in the world.

As you become wiser, your life just gets better.

My purpose is to inspire you to seek wisdom in your daily life, because life is always teaching. The question is: are you willing to listen and learn? The topics I cover in this book are simply things I have been inspired to share. I am not a know-all, be-all voice. I'm just a person who has grown to understand the power of wisdom in our lives. I only want to share things that have had a positive influence on my life. My goal is not to tell you what to think, but what to think about. This book is about helping you grow as a person.

Wise people understand that it is the simple things in life that are extraordinary.

Throughout my life, things have happened to me—life experiences that have shaped how I wanted to live. They were simple things that made a big impact. My hope is to take those life lessons and relate them to you in a way that will help you grow and improve your life.

It's not just the big moments that change our lives. The simple and obvious things can teach us our most valuable lessons if we pay attention. We spend our life in search of answers. We think we'll find them in some new discovery, some formula for living. The result is that we miss the obvious answers that life can provide in our daily experiences.

Wisdom exists in our everyday life. It can be found in the books we read, the conversations we have with strangers or loved ones, and in the stories and songs we hear. At its core, life is pretty simple. The answer we seek is usually obvious, but we tend to overlook obvious things in our search. We discover wisdom by living and growing as a human being. The potential for finding wisdom is unlimited. We will never soak it all in, but we can continue to drink from the well. Nothing makes life more refreshing and exciting than a beautiful, fresh cup of wisdom. Just like a cup of cold water on a hot Georgia day, it gives you new energy and appreciation for the magnificence of life.

In my life, I have been blessed to have met and worked with some of the smartest, most influential leaders in financial services. I have met famous athletes, politicians, and thought leaders on multiple topics. I am an avid reader on a broad range of subjects and have read over a thousand books. I have always been in a position of leadership and have been blessed to work with extraordinary teams. But as I reflect back on my life, I am surprised to discover that though these influences played a role, they are not the primary factors that have guided and directed my life.

Some of the most influential factors in my life turned out to be maxims.

A maxim is a statement expressing a general truth or rule of conduct, and my life has been guided by a series of them. They contain simple powerful words that have blessed my life when followed and caused my life to get off track when ignored. When I started this project, I was surprised to discover that the maxims that have guided my life did not come from books or famous people. They came from family, friends, personal acquaintances, and everyday life experiences.

As I live the next phase of my life, I hope to become a wiser man. One maxim that I believe is, "You reap what you sow." So, for me to become wiser, and to help others become wiser too, I believe I must sow seeds of wisdom. The seeds I am led to sow are the maxims I have learned from people who spent a lifetime living by them. I thank God they took the time to share them with me. Now I hope to share them with you and make a difference for you and your life.

In my life, I have been called a wise old owl, a coach, "Forrest Gump," and full of crap. I am proud to have earned any or all of these titles, and I have learned lessons in all of those roles. As you read this book, you will probably see a little of all these names coming through in my message. If you do, be open-minded to the idea that there might be a touch of wisdom—maybe a pearl—that will help make your life a little better.

I did not write this book to try to change the world, although that would be nice. I am writing because I felt led to do it. This is an odd statement, coming from someone who never wrote a term paper while he was in college. And I bet there is no evidence I ever wrote a memo over the course of my thirty-six-year career. I answered most of my emails with "Give me a call," or "Let's discuss," so this writing endeavor is out of character for me. But when you are led to do something, you have to have the courage to take action and make it happen.

There are two things to note as you read this book.

One thing is that I will use the word "man" throughout the book because I learned the lessons as a man, but the intent is that the word will apply to all human beings. The maxims you're about to read are meant to have significance for all people—regardless of sex, color, creed, religion, or sexual orientation. The second thing is that I will give no credit for quotes or ideas. Nobody's ego needs to be stroked—these ideas and words just need to be shared. I don't know where most of the quotes came from. Ultimately, I believe, they come from God. Remember, Solomon was right: There is nothing new under the sun. But feel free to claim your idea or quote and take it with you on your journey to wisdom.

Let's get rolling!

Introduction

BEGINNING THE SEARCH
FOR WISDOM

THE SEARCH FOR WISDOM BEGINS with the fundamentals. The great coaches I have studied do not assume anything. They start with the fundamentals. Vince Lombardi, the great NFL coach, would start his first practice of the season with "Gentlemen, this is a football." The great college basketball coach John Wooden would start the season showing his players the proper way to put on basketball socks and shoes to avoid blisters. This book covers the fundamentals from my life's playbook. No matter how wise you are, it never hurts to be reminded of what you know.

Let's start with the first fundamental or maxim we must all come to terms with—there is a God, and it is not you. You might have talent, and you might have wisdom, but whatever you have at the moment is not equal to your full potential. To move closer to your potential, you must look up. And as you merge your God-given talents with God's wisdom, your life just gets better.

Why Should We Search for Wisdom?

When I was a kid, I loved the story of Solomon establishing himself as the king of Israel. God appeared to Solomon in a dream and asked Solomon what he should give him. Solomon could have asked for anything in the world, but he asked for wisdom.

Now imagine you are twenty years old, and your father is King David—a great warrior. Your father chooses you as his successor over your older brothers, but when he dies, nobody believes you have any business being king except your mother, your deceased father, and your God. To top it off, God appears and tells you he will give you whatever you ask for. Your answer will determine your fate and the fate of a nation. Now the magnitude of this moment pales in compares to anything I have faced in my sixty-three years of life. With the weight of the world on his young and inexperienced shoulders, Solomon chose wisdom, and the rest is history. He reigned as king for forty years in the most prosperous period in Israel's history. Not only did God bless Solomon with the wisdom to rule a nation, He also blessed him with honor and wealth beyond his wildest dreams.

As a kid, I would contemplate whether Solomon asked for the right thing. If God were to grant me one answered prayer, what would I ask for? Fame, fortune, power, athletic ability, or wisdom? My dream was to be an NFL quarterback like Fran

Tarkenton. If I could scramble, run, and pass like Fran, I could have it all. I also considered whether the answer was to ask for wealth. If I had an unlimited supply of money, could I solve all the world's problems? But as I thought about these questions, they always led me down a pig path to nowhere (this is a southern expression that means following a path in the woods that leads to a dead end). I was never smart enough to come up with a better answer. As I have gotten older, and hopefully, a little wiser, I realize that Solomon's prayer for wisdom was the ultimate answer.

Throughout my life, I have prayed for wisdom. I was never able to let go of the fact that it worked for Solomon, and I thought it might just work for me. In reality, time after time, I did what I wanted to do instead of what I knew was right. I would mess my life up and pray to God for the wisdom to clean it up.

The more I focus on wisdom when tackling life's opportunities and challenges, the better my life gets. I am a long way from the wisdom of Solomon, but I do believe that with wisdom comes strength, courage, energy, and enthusiasm. Most importantly, wisdom leads to loving God, loving people, and loving life.

Regardless of your personal beliefs, we all have to explore our own unique journey for wisdom. It doesn't matter who you are or what you believe—the only absolute I will state is that there is a God, and it is not you. I believe that for us to have life, and have it abundantly, we must be on a personal spiritual journey. As we seek wisdom, our spiritual lives will grow, and all aspects of our lives will improve.

The more time and effort you spend on this personal journey, the better your life will be. Solomon, the man who earned the title of the wisest man who ever lived, started his journey by asking his Creator for wisdom. He changed his life by seeking wisdom. He did not delay to some future date; he took action in the moment. Wisdom is always calling. It is up to us to answer the call. Is there a better time to answer the call than right now?

As a kid, I dreamed of being an NFL quarterback or a major league second baseman. I was a good high school athlete, lettering in baseball, football, and basketball. By my senior year, I was five feet eight inches tall and only weighed a hundred and thirty pounds. I like to think I got the most out of my talent. But it was not enough to accomplish my dreams. It was clear life was headed in another direction. While I attended college, and during my work life, I interacted with so many people who were much more intelligent and talented than I was. School and business were the same as sports; we were not created with the same talents. Like with sports, I was always looking for an edge or a great equalizer. In the classroom, I got good grades by listening to the professors and spending my time on what mattered. I was better than most at studying what would be on the exams. I could not retain and recall information like my classmates with exceptional IQs. Later, in business, I would sit in meetings with these folks who were smarter than the average bear, but not that good at coming up with creative, viable solutions to our opportunities and challenges. They were more knowledgeable than I was, but I could go toe-to-toe with them on making wise decisions. The more I looked up for answers, the better decisions I made, regardless of my talent level or the talent level of people around me.

The Power of Wisdom

But I discovered two things about the power of wisdom in all areas of life. First, people who have God-given talents don't necessarily become wise people who end up living happy and fulfilling lives. And second, wisdom seems to flow equally to all who seek it. It's a lot like sunshine. It's there for all of us, but some people take advantage of wisdom more than others. Wisdom, like sunshine, doesn't care whether you are smart or good-looking, or whether you can run fast. Wisdom is abundantly available to all who seek it.

MAXIM 1
There is a God, and it is not you.

Spend time on your personal journey. Don't do what most of us do, which is spend just two or three seconds in prayer and meditation. It amazes me how little time I spend each day on the most important aspect of life—the soul. The more time you spend seeking spiritual wisdom and direction, the better your life will be. So, you have to put your game plan together and decide when during each day you will seek spiritual guidance— the more, the better. Don't miss this point. You won't find the answers or be the best you can be without looking up and connecting to a power outside yourself.

QUESTIONS TO PONDER:

1. When you think about a power bigger than yourself, what do you think about?

2. On your journey to become wiser, can you see yourself connecting to and relying on a power outside yourself?

PART ONE

Maxims from

MOM

MY MOTHER HAS ALWAYS BEEN our family's moral compass. She taught us right from wrong. She has lived her life by giving unconditional love, never complaining, always sacrificing, and doing her best for her family. Even to this day, my mother's unconditional love sets her apart from everyone I have known.

She spent her childhood in Atlanta, but when she was in the seventh grade, she moved with her family to the small town of Grayson, Georgia. My father returned home from World War II and spent a short time in civilian life, then he re-enlisted in the army. While Dad was home on leave, Mom's sister was dating a friend of Dad's, and she arranged for them to meet. They started dating, fell in love, and decided to get married before Dad shipped out to Korea. Mom was only seventeen when Dad left again for another war, and she started living the life of an army wife. When he returned, they were stationed in multiple locations. My sister Jeanie was born in Texas. My brother Lee and I were born in Germany. My youngest brother Stan was born in Tennessee. Mom had to take care of us with no family support, moving when and where Uncle Sam wanted her to. Her last stop as a military wife was Colorado Springs, Colorado.

At that time, Dad had served twenty years in the army and was eligible to retire. As the story goes, Mom made the decision for him. Vietnam was heating up, and he had fought in two wars. He'd done his part. She was not seeing him off to another war. He retired, and we moved back to Grayson to be near their families. She raised her kids, took care of her parents in their final days, worked as a secretary at the elementary school, and then retired from the U.S. Postal Service. One of her biggest joys after retirement was spending time with her grandkids. Mom taught two generations right from wrong by her example. She was humble, yet strong, and she always appreciated the blessings life brought her way.

Mom did not take no for an answer; instead, she had an incredible way of helping you be a better person. You always knew when Mom gave you advice that she had your best interest at heart. Now I was a far cry from a mama's boy. In fact, I spent most of my time with Dad, but I realize now what a powerful, positive influence my mother had on me and my life. Her words and her example form the core of who I am.

Mom's words provided me with so much wisdom. There were three maxims that she used that have guided my life through the good times and the bad. The way she lived her life exemplifies these words:

Do the right thing, and the rest will come out in the wash.

Can't never could.

If ifs and ands were pots and pans, you would not have to buy any.

These three maxims have been invaluable in my search for wisdom.

DO THE RIGHT THING, AND THE REST WILL COME OUT IN THE WASH

ONE OF THE GREATEST PIECES of wisdom I received in my life was from my mom. I usually did not talk things over with her; I always talked to my dad. Dad was my best friend, my rock, and my go-to person. But one day, for whatever reason, Dad was not immediately available, so I went to Mom. I don't remember what I was struggling with, I only remember what she said: "Do the right thing, and the rest will come out in the wash."

Mom did not tell me what to think, she gave me what I should think *about*. She did not explain right from wrong. She provided a guiding principle that would point me in the right direction. She didn't make the decision for me but helped me realize that once I made the decision, there would be consequences, and I had to deal with those consequences. If the consequences of your decision broke a few eggs, you had to clean up the mess.

Life requires us to make decisions constantly. When we make wise decisions, our life improves—even if it's only in the short term we have to sail though choppy water. The wise people I know don't run from decisions—they make them. Also, they get good at improving the quality of their decisions, and they master the execution once the decision is made. They anticipate the consequences, especially the impact their decision will have on people. The most important part of execution is anticipating how others will feel about what you decided. While they may not like it, if they know you are attempting to do the right thing, there is a higher possibility they will accept it.

When you are struggling to make a decision, do the right thing, and the rest will come out in the wash. In my life, whenever I have struggled with what I should do, I think about Mom's advice. When I followed my conscience, which I've always called my heart, and did what I believed at the time to be the right thing, I never regretted it. When I chose not to do what my heart was telling me, things got worse.

When I am faced with a decision, big or small, I put Mom's advice at the top of my guiding principles. This maxim works with any decision in any area of your life. Most of our decisions do not involve life and death. Sometimes, to get perspective, I reflect back on the generals in the Civil War—men like Ulysses S. Grant, Robert E. Lee, William Tecumseh Sherman, and Stonewall Jackson. These were men who had tens of thousands of men under their command, and when they gave the order to attack in a major battle, it was a given that thousands would die. It was brother against brother, countryman against countryman.

To me, this type of decision is the ultimate in knowing what the right thing is, and knowing the consequences of your decision. Do nothing, men die; do what you believe is the right thing, men die. Thank goodness, for most of us, the decisions we make today will not be life or death, but many of the decisions we make will impact people and there will be consequences for us and for others. Your decisions matter to you—and to others.

There is an old country song that had a line something like "shall I turn left or right at Main Street—that's the choice I make each day." The message is go left and run away from your job, your family, and all your responsibilities. Go right and do your job, take care of your family, and embrace your responsibilities. Using Mom's maxim as our guide, most of us make the choice to turn right, and the consequences are that we go to work, make decisions, and come home to our families. In reality, we are making decisions on a moment-to-moment basis. Those decisions will determine our life's journey and will have a significant impact on others. If I had followed Mom's advice 100 percent of the time, there is no doubt my life and the lives of others would have been exponentially better. The wise are consistent; they strive to do the right thing, always examining their understanding of what the right thing truly is. They anticipate the impact of their decisions on others. They make the right decision to the best of their ability. They deal with both the intended consequences and the unintended consequences. Life's a little like laundry—even with the best of intentions, you're going to get some stains on your clothes. But in most cases, these will get cleaned up in the wash.

Sometimes There Are No Perfect Answers

Like the decisions of those generals, some decisions have no perfect answer. Here's the thing: being wise is about making good decisions, and making those decisions for the right reasons. It is also about understanding the consequences of those decisions. Many of our mistakes in life occur when we try to avoid the consequences of doing the right thing. Sometimes, there are no perfect answers to life's challenges.

As you make decisions, always ask yourself, *Am I making this decision based on my own best interests, or the best interests of others?* In today's society, people are more focused on their self-interest than at any time I can remember. Maybe it's just that as I have gotten a little older, I am more aware. The young leaders I work with today approach every situation asking what they stand to personally gain. Now, I'm not here to pass judgment. They might know something I don't. What's important is to be aware it's happening. I grew up playing team sports where the leaders put the team first. In today's sports, athletes put their playing time, stats, and ego above the team. You see the same thing in business. The question isn't, "What can I do to make the business better?" It's "When am I going to get a raise?" or "When am I going get promoted?" Strive for clarity regarding your motives. Then ask yourself, *Am I really making the decision for the right reasons?* Wisdom is action. It is doing the right thing for the right reasons and having the courage and faith to trust the outcome. It's not always easy to know which way to go, but you have to believe that life ultimately rewards those who do the right thing.

Now here is the thing with tough decisions—sometimes right and wrong get all balled up together. There was a great scene in the movie *Get Low* with Robert Duvall. He was explaining why he lied about what happened one night when a married woman he loved died in a house fire. He wanted to protect her reputation, so he lied about what happened. To explain why he lied, he said there is right and there is wrong in life, but sometimes they get balled up together. In the scene, he balled his fingers together. He was faced with having to make a decision about what to say when there wasn't any perfect answer. And he ultimately lied to protect the reputation of someone he loved. Did he do the right thing? Is it okay to lie to protect people you love? Sometimes tough decisions need wisdom that is only available to those who look up for the answer. The wise person understands that there is a source greater than themselves that opens up to those who seek it.

Decisions involving people are always the toughest. There will be someone who doesn't get promoted, who doesn't make the team, whose reputation is changed. These decisions affect people at a deeper level than most of us ever think. When you make a decision to promote someone to a leadership position, the only person who may like the decision is the person you promoted. Their peers believe *they* deserved the promotion, regardless of the facts. Never take for granted what others are thinking and feeling. If you sense someone will be upset with a decision you are making, have an individual conversation with them before you make a public announcement. Always treat others with respect when you implement your decision. A wise decision poorly implemented is a bad decision. Once you make a tough decision involving people, the work is just beginning. Don't avoid these tough conversations. While they might be difficult, it will be more than worth it.

The beauty of life is that if you follow your heart and do the right thing to the best of your ability, things seem to work themselves out. People might not like your decision, but if they know you and know you took the time and effort to do the right thing, they will tend to accept and understand it.

When you are dealing with tough decisions, I suggest the following actions:

1. Pray for direction.

2. Sleep on your decision. For me, life is clearer at the start of a new day.

3. Follow your heart. Your thoughts can mislead you, but your heart never will.

Making the Right (or Wrong) Decision

Making good decisions is about seeing things as they are, not as we want them to be—and having the courage to act appropriately. We have a tendency to not want to deal with reality, so we ignore it. In business, when sales start trending downward, we think it will only be temporary, so we delay taking action, and the downward trend continues.

When my youngest son Matt fell off the monkey bars, I thought he had bruised his arm. But my wife Trisha saw reality—Matt's arm was broken. Not seeing and dealing with reality can keep us from making wise decisions. It was obvious in hindsight that Matt needed to be checked by a doctor. The wiser we become, the better we see and respond to reality versus wishful thinking. You must have the courage to face reality and act in response to it. Once you get your arms around the issue, it won't get better until you take action. If it is a significant decision, focus on the wisdom of doing the right thing. You will know it's what you are supposed to do when your heart, your head, your instincts, and your guidance from above are all leading you in the same direction. I make my final decisions with the dawning of a new day. For me, the early morning is the clearest time to see where life is leading me. Don't keep putting the decision off. Deal with it and take action. Even with the best of intentions, however, we sometimes make the wrong decision. When this happens, apologize to those who have been negatively impacted.

At my former company, we did on-stage recognition of MVPs every two years at our international convention—in front of forty to fifty thousand people. We would spend hours making decisions and reviewing production numbers to make sure we did not miss anyone. Inevitably we would make a bad decision in our selection criteria, and we would miss someone who deserved to be recognized. Typically, we would discover the mistake based on a conversation with the person after the event. Once the event was over, all we could do was admit our mistake and apologize. It is a tough conversation to have, but if the person you've offended knows the heart and effort that went into the decision, they are more likely to forgive you. Learn from your mistake, and try not to make the same mistake twice. Experience is the greatest teacher.

MAXIM 2

Do the right thing, and the rest will come out in the wash.

Your decisions determine your character and impact the quality and direction of your life and the lives of others. Your decision making will improve if it is guided by the right principles. Put doing the right thing at the top of your guiding principles, and the results will change your life. Be wise. Do the right thing, and the rest will come out in the wash.

QUESTIONS TO PONDER:

1. Today, what decisions do you need to make that require wisdom and courage to do the right thing?

2. Do you feel limited by a lack of courage?

3. How can you find the strength and courage to do the right thing?

4. Are you prepared to deal with the consequences of your decision?

CAN'T NEVER COULD

WHEN WE WERE KIDS, IF we ever said we couldn't do something, Mom would remind us that "can't never could." You hear all your life that you are a product of your environment. Mom created an environment where she consistently reinforced this idea of persistence. If she was helping me with my spelling homework, and I said, "I can't spell that word," her response was, "Can't never could." She would constantly remind me that I *could* spell it, but it was going to take a little more time and effort to actually do it. She didn't yell or scream or threaten to punish me. She planted seeds of belief and work ethic. Mom was a master of persistence. Not spelling that word was just not an option. I had to stay after it until it got done. I use this example because I hated spelling. I struggle with it to this day. Thank God for the new technology. Now the spelling of any word is in the palm of your hand.

Throughout my early life, Mom told me time after time that I could do things, even when my first efforts were unsuccessful.

Learning to swim, riding a bicycle, hitting a baseball—the list is endless. The constant was Mom's reminders that can't never could. Don't quit. Put forth a little more time and effort. You can do it. As a young athlete, I was always one of the smallest players. I would look around at the people I had to compete with for play-time and start to doubt whether I had any business even trying. But I knew one thing—can't never could. So, I would compete to the best of my ability knowing it would take time, effort, and a lot of hustle, but the only way to find out what I was truly capable of was to go for it.

In my work life, I made a career out of taking on new challenges. When my responsibilities expanded, it usually came down to the fact that those who were making the decision may have had doubts about my abilities, but they did not have a better choice. They knew I wouldn't tick off the people who ran the day-to-day operation, and that I wouldn't mess things up while they looked for the right person. But thanks to Mom's maxim, I turned my focus to believing I could do it versus doubting my abilities. So I would hit the ground running, not having a clue what I was doing, but never doubting I could do it. I was always blessed to work with wonderful people who responded to my leadership. I will hang my hat on the fact that every area I led was left better than I found it—thanks to Mom's wisdom.

Mom's words have stuck with me throughout my life—probably to a fault. Anytime I attempt something, and I struggle to do it, it just burns my butt. My family will always think twice before asking me to do something, simply because if things don't go right, I am hard to live with. I have always had a bit of a temper when things don't go my way. I have worked on it my entire life. If

I attempted to do something—win a backyard football game, put together a toy—I would cuss, fight, and carry on like a crazy man.

One Christmas when my sons Chess and Matt were in elementary school, Mom and my wife Trisha were buying them a trampoline. When the salesperson asked if they wanted to pay fifty dollars to have it delivered and installed, they answered "yes" in unison. It would be worth fifty dollars not to have to listen to me while I was putting it together. That was a good coaching moment for me. It made me aware that I sometimes took things two steps too far. Mom's maxim did not include being a horse's ass.

But in spite of how I responded to Mom's lesson, it is still valuable. Anything you want to attempt in life can only be done if you believe you can do it. Most of us have such a limited belief in what we are capable of doing. I think we all battle with this. We put limits on what we can do to avoid how uncomfortable the unknown makes us feel. We never consider that life doesn't always set limits on our success—most of the time we set the limits ourselves. We never consider all the things that are limitless—wisdom, love, faith, courage, energy—things that give us what we need to accomplish more on our life's journey.

One of the most limiting things in my life is my lack of self-belief in certain areas. I have not always followed Mom's maxim. I never thought I was a good public speaker. For most of my career, I avoided opportunities to grow in this area. This limited my career and the impact I had on the lives of others in the company. I set the boundaries of what was possible. We have a tendency to avoid the things that scare us, the things that make us uncomfortable. These fears make us less than what we can be.

Becoming aware of the limitations of *can't* and the power of *can* sets life on a more fulfilling trajectory. As we become wiser, we see this more clearly. If there is something you need to do, or something you want to do, the only way it will get done is for you to believe you can do it. If your starting point is *can't*, you are destined to never start, but if you start with *can*, there is not much in life that can't be done. There may be plenty in life that we're not very good at—at least in the beginning. But believing you can do it is a powerful starting point.

MAXIM 3
Can't never could.

Can't is a word that limits your life. *Can* is a word that empowers your life. Get good at replacing *can't* with *can* and see your life change in ways you never thought possible.

QUESTIONS TO PONDER:

1. Today, can you think of a situation where *can't* is stopping you from doing what you need to do, or what you are called to do?

2. Or can you think of past situations where *can't* stopped you?

3. What can you do going forward to remove this barrier?

IF *IFS* AND *ANDS* WERE POTS AND PANS, YOU WOULD NOT HAVE TO BUY ANY

WHEN WE WERE KIDS, MY mother never liked it when we made excuses for not doing what we were supposed to. Anytime we tried to make excuses, she would listen for the words "if" and "and," and when we said them, she would say, "If *ifs* and *ands* were pots and pans, you would not have to buy any." Mom had learned this from her mother who had modified the saying "If *ifs* and *ands* were pots and pans, there'd be no work for tinkers' hands." My family's modified version of the saying comes to my mind anytime I catch myself making excuses.

One of the wisest quotes on the subject is, "You can make excuses, or you can get results, but you can't do both." Nothing will get your life off track faster than excuses. Guard against them like the plague. To live wisely, you must constantly be summoning up the courage to act. Taking action is the only way you'll be able to make the most out of your life. Sure, it's easy to think of excuses for not doing what you know you should. And there will never be the perfect set of circumstances. But anytime you catch yourself making excuses, replace them with thoughts about the solution. Start to pay attention to the excuses you make for not doing something. I was always amazed when I was given a new area of responsibility at work. I would meet with the leadership, and they would spend their time making excuses about why things were not going as well as they should have been.

"If we had more money in the budget, we could get more programming resources."

"If we had more people, we would improve our ability to serve our clients and sales force."

The excuses would go on and on. When I asked them what they were doing about it, their response was typically something along the lines of, "There is nothing we can do." My response would be, "You might be right, but let's focus our time and attention on solutions—not why something can't be done, but how we're going to get it done." We proposed and implemented amazing creative ideas and impactful plans by changing our conversations from excuses to solutions.

Throughout my career, the most unproductive business meetings were the ones where everyone spent all their time and energy focusing on why something could not be done. The most productive meetings I ran or attended were focused on the solutions, not the problems. Wise people don't give a damn about what can't be done. They focus on what needs to be done and how to get it done. Wise people know that solutions arise from creativity and excuses arise from fear. This is true in all areas of your life.

Whatever you focus on grows. If you focus on why something can't be done, all you will have is more excuses. If you are thinking, *If I had more time*, or *If I had more money*—you name it—instead of thinking about how you will accomplish your objective, you are wasting valuable time and energy on fruitless efforts. A wiser approach would be to focus on creative solutions. If in fact the best or only answer is more time or money, focus on how you will get them and don't spend your time wishing you had them.

Ifs and *ands* will not get you the results you want.

Wise people also know that they have the ability to find answers by tapping into the power of their Creator. There is this infinite source that will lead you to the answers and the actions that life desires of you. Look up, because the answers you seek are closer than you think. Don't let *ifs* and *ands* stop you.

MAXIM 4

If ifs *and* ands *were pots and pans, you would not have to buy any.*

A wise person knows excuses don't get results.

QUESTIONS TO PONDER:

1. What is an excuse you've been using lately or have used in the past that has stopped you from pursuing or achieving the results you want?

2. When dealing with life's opportunities and challenges, how will you change your focus when you find yourself making excuses?

PART TWO

Maxims from
DAD

I ALWAYS LOVED BEING WITH my dad. He passed away in 2012. While I try to keep moving forward rather than looking back, I find myself feeling his presence almost daily. To this day, I have a desire to make my dad proud. I never wanted to disappoint him, and when I did, it broke my heart. He was a person in my life whose opinion I truly cared about. He was the person I always went to when I needed someone to talk to. His wide range of life experiences gave him a unique perspective. He had a way of helping you know what you should think about, but he expected you to make the decision. Once I made a decision, he was always there to help and support me in any way he could.

He lived through the Great Depression and believed from childhood to death that life had blessed him with everything materially he needed to be happy. He always said he "lived the life of Riley." He served twenty years in the U.S. Army and fought in World War II and the Korean Conflict. He retired and opened a fast food restaurant in Snellville, Georgia, that became a gathering place for the community. He typified the Greatest Generation.

He had seen the best of life and the worst of life. In World War II, he served in the 3rd Armored Division. They landed in France eighteen days after D-Day and fought through the entire European Campaign. He experienced the reality of war. He saw death and suffering and the liberation of a Nazi concentration camp. Through it all, he developed a unique perspective on life. He loved life, loved people, and always saw the best in those around him. He helped me realize that the things I struggled with were manageable—but that other people had real challenges to face. One year we were in Lexington watching the University of Georgia play Kentucky in football. We were with four or five of Dad's friends who were complaining about how cold it was. Now, by Southern standards, it was cold. We were sitting in the upper deck. The wind was blowing like a freight train. Between the wind and the temperature and us not being dressed for the weather, we were cold. Dad looked at me and said, "Son, this ain't cold. Cold is eating your Christmas Eve dinner in a snow-covered foxhole in Europe." That was Dad's way of making the point that what we were feeling was nothing compared to the coldest day of his life. This was not that bad, physically or emotionally. We were watching a football game. We were doing something we loved, not enduring the realities of war on Christmas Eve like he and his fellow soldiers had. Suffering is relative, and when you put things into perspective, most of our struggles are not that big of a deal. That's how Dad looked at life.

He taught me to love life, to be thankful for what I had, and to look for the best in others. Mom was our moral compass, and Dad taught us people skills for life. He got along with people from all walks of life and made friends with everyone he met.

Three maxims from Dad's life are these:

The bed is your enemy.

Beware of living one paycheck away from disaster.

Death is our greatest teacher.

THE BED IS YOUR ENEMY

WHEN I WAS IN HIGH school, I played three sports, worked at my dad's fast-food restaurant, and always had other summer jobs. On the weekends, I was looking to have fun. That could mean going hunting or fishing during the day or going out at night.

One weekend morning, I decided to sleep in. It was probably about ten in the morning when my dad came in and said, "You get up early all week to go to school, play ball, and work. Today you have a free day to play, and your choice is to lie in bed. That makes no sense to me." That morning, I still lay in bed, but I couldn't get the words out of my head. As a young man, I finally turned those words into action. I always aim to rise early every day, whether it's work or play, excited about the day—especially on a day I can play.

My point here is that sometimes we tend to lie in bed dreading the day. There is something about the waking hour that makes us worry about the day versus being excited about it.

For me, if I can hit the ground running, all those worries get smaller or disappear completely. I love the line from the movie *Secondhand Lions*, "You want to die with your boots on." That's the way I want to go. Not lying in bed dreading the day. Life is so short and so precious. Don't waste it. I also love the line from the Jimmy Buffet song that talks about there being still so much to be done. Life has so much to offer. Don't lie in bed when life is calling you to hit the ground running. Be wise and know when your internal clock or alarm clock goes off, it's time to wake up, roll out of bed, and be excited and grateful for another day.

I share these wise words from Proverbs 6:6–11 to illustrate what I mean:

> *Go to the ant, O sluggard;*
> *consider her ways, and be wise.*
> *Without having any chief, officer, or ruler,*
> *She prepares her food in summer,*
> *And gathers her sustenance in harvest.*
> *How long will you lie there, O sluggard?*
> *When will you arise from your sleep?*
> *A little sleep, a little slumber,*
> *a little folding of the hands to rest,*
> *and poverty will come upon you like a vagabond,*
> *and want like an armed man.*

Regardless of how talented or how blessed we are, I believe God gave all of us an unlimited amount of spiritual energy. Those of us who are not blessed with exceptional physical or mental abilities must rely on this spiritual energy. Think about something you love to do: going to a ballgame, going to the beach, spending time with a grandchild. What would happen if you came home from work on a Friday evening, dead tired, and your best friend had two tickets to see your favorite team play for a championship, or two plane tickets to your favorite beach destination? What if your grandchild was at your house? Your energy level would soar. Where does this unlimited energy come from? I believe it comes from above. It is available to us at any time at any hour of the day. We open our hearts, and energy pours in. We close our hearts to the source, and our batteries are drained. This energy is available for all areas of your life, not just for the things you love.

Yesterday I helped my son Matt move to a new apartment. Moving is not my favorite thing in life to say the least, but I was able to hit the ground running. I drove two hours to Macon, Georgia, worked twelve hours, and drove two hours home. The day flew by. It was actually fun figuring out how to move some furniture that I initially thought would require some help. Life is energy: We must be wise enough to find the source and be open to receiving its bountiful supply. To me, that is the great equalizer. People can say you're not very talented, but they should never be able to question your heart, your hustle, or your energy.

When I played baseball in high school, I was not the most talented, but I believed nobody should have more energy or hustle than me. Between innings, I always wanted to be the first player on and off the field. When my energy level was high, my performance improved. The great women's basketball coach Pat Summitt believed with hustle and effort you can beat a more talented team. As we become wiser, our energy level rises, and our performance in all areas improves. When the sun comes up, hit the ground running.

MAXIM 5

The bed is your enemy.

When it's time to rise, don't delay. At that moment, the bed is your enemy.

QUESTIONS TO PONDER:

1. This morning, did you hit the ground running?

2. If you didn't, do you know why?

3. Can you describe what you feel when the bed is your source of rest?

4. How is it different from the times you lie in bed wasting the morning and dreading the day?

BEWARE OF LIVING ONE PAYCHECK AWAY FROM DISASTER

I WAS BLESSED WITH WONDERFUL parents. Because my dad was raised during the Great Depression, he always had a conservative approach toward money. He hated debt, but he knew how to use it wisely. When he got out of the army and opened his restaurant, he worked hard, long hours, and over time, the business became successful. It provided a means to educate his kids and a good retirement for him and my mom.

Every day, he would count the money and get his deposit ready for the bank. As I got older, I noticed we had the means to have a bigger house and a better car. One day, when Dad was getting his deposit ready, I asked him how all these other people were able to afford big houses and nicer cars. He looked at me and said we can afford those things too, but most of those people are one paycheck away from disaster. Those words stuck with me for the rest of my life. I knew at that moment that I did not want to live one paycheck away from losing everything.

As I became an adult, his wise words have guided me in my approach to money. Anytime I make a financial decision, I make sure that I can afford it, and it does not put undue strain on my family's finances.

Money is a funny thing—It can be a blessing and a curse. With money, you can do wonderful things for yourself and others. But money can also hurt you and others. One day, I was in downtown Atlanta for work. I had some free time, so I took a walk. A lady who appeared homeless and hungry asked me for money. Thinking I was doing the right thing, I gave her twenty dollars. I walked a few more steps, and a guy who knew the lady screamed at me, "What are you doing? You probably killed her." It turns out she was a drug addict, and I'd just paid for her next fix. With those twenty dollars, did I bless or curse that lady? How we handle our money matters. This was a vivid reminder that I should be wise with what I do with money. Even giving away a small amount can be a double-edged sword.

In reality, your family and the other causes you support are better served when you have money and handle it wisely. I would like to share four rules that have helped me financially. Given your current situation these may seem impossible or impractical. They certainly did when I was making $850 a month, as well as when I had my best annual income ever. Regardless of where you are financially, you should consider the wisdom of these rules. For me—and probably for you—the important thing is to get started doing something. With money, the sooner you start, the better your odds of success.

Rule 1

GIVE AWAY 10 PERCENT OF EVERY DOLLAR YOU MAKE.

It takes a leap of faith. It's not logical. My financial situation never improved until I began working on Rule 1. Giving it away means giving and expecting nothing in return. This is not a prosperity message. It's a giving message. Be a gracious giver; don't give begrudgingly. Give a heartfelt gift for one purpose—to bless others.

Rule 2

SAVE A MINIMUM OF 10 PERCENT AND LIVE ON THE REST.

Hopefully you will start at 10 percent, grow that percentage as your income grows, and you will live within your means. This will put you in a position to never be one paycheck away from a disaster of your own making. If you have a financial disaster, it will be because of an extraordinary event beyond your control. Saving money gives you choices in life. Like it or not, money is important. If used wisely, money can improve your life and the lives of others.

Rule 3

BE WISE ABOUT HOW YOU USE DEBT.

I am no expert on debt, nor am I the person to give you advice on specifics. But I do know debt used foolishly will destroy you emotionally and financially—so be wise about it. Debt can make you a prisoner, and a life without it can give you freedom. Sometimes it's a necessary evil, but it has real consequences. Use it wisely, or—if possible—not at all. Be careful of what you own, or it will own you.

Rule 4

PAY YOUR TAXES.

There are laws to protect you from every creditor except Uncle Sam. A debt to him is the one debt that is never forgiven. He is going to get his money, plus interest and penalties, and once you are in his web, you cannot get out. Don't let him get on your back. Ask anyone who is trying to get Uncle Sam off his or her back. It is almost impossible.

MAXIM 6
Beware of living one paycheck away from disaster.

That three-minute conversation with Dad about why we did not live in a bigger house or drive a better car helped me understand that money is a blessing, and you should use it wisely. Beware of the burden of living one paycheck away from disaster. Remember that money is a terrible master but a valuable servant. Use your financial blessings wisely.

QUESTIONS TO PONDER:

1. Can you think of a time when money was a terrible master?

2. Is debt straining your monthly cash flow?

3. Are you living one paycheck away from disaster?

4. Are you making financial decisions that are guided by wise financial principles?

DEATH IS OUR
GREATEST TEACHER

EVERY FUNERAL I'VE ATTENDED AND every death I've
mourned since I was a young kid has taught me great lessons
about life. With every loss of someone I've loved, I have drawn
strength and wisdom from their lives. When I was eleven years
old, I lost my Papaw—Walt Britt. It was my first experience
with death. I remember learning of his death like it was yesterday. After the initial shock, even at that young age, all I
could think about was how he taught me so much and how
much better my life was because of him. He gave me my first
lesson in hitting a baseball. He had a key to the Grayson gym
and taught his grandkids the fundamentals of basketball. He
was the first person I worked for, and he demanded I do my
best. I could write a whole book just on lessons from Papaw.
When my dad died, his grandkids asked me to speak at the
funeral. It was the first time I put into words the lessons I had
learned from the life of someone I loved. My dad was more

than just a loved one; he was my rock and my best friend in life. At the funeral, I spoke to the grandkids about the lessons learned from their Papaw's life:

1. Love your family, no matter what.

2. Everything will be all right. The good Lord will take care of things, no matter what happens in life.

3. Soldier on when things get tough.

4. Approach life with excitement and enthusiasm. It doesn't matter the circumstances: a football game, a vacation, a meal with your family, or even a cold Coca-Cola.

5. Be optimistic and expect the best. It doesn't matter whether it's a ball game or a family crisis.

6. Love people, and accept them for who they are.

7. When the sun comes up, hit the ground running. (My dad's life was eighty-seven years of perpetual motion.)

8. Work hard, but enjoy life. Look forward to the next adventure regardless of whether it's big or small. Be excited about life.

My dad loved going to Daytona Beach, Florida, on vacation. But as much as he loved going, he loved being excited about the trip just as much. The anticipation of the trip fueled him with energy for months. He was the same way about anything in life. He saw the wisdom of always looking forward to whatever life had to offer. We are only on this earth for a short time. Love life. Be happy. I pray we would all have my dad's enthusiasm for life. Wisdom is loving life, counting your blessings, and hitting the ground running each day to make the most of life.

As we try to make the most of every day, we are wise to remember that death is the great equalizer regardless of who you are, where you come from, how much money you have, or what you believe. We come into the world with nothing, and we will leave with nothing. In life, as in the game of chess, when the game is over, the king and the pawn go back in the same box.

As with everything in life, the end is always closer than you think—never forget this. No one knows when or how death will come. Live your life as if this day were your last. Know that eternity is a reality. One of the biggest issues we face in life is our understanding of death. Do we fear it or do we respect it? Death is the thing that makes life so precious. Because death is so unpredictable, we never know when our time is up. My Papaw died fishing at Lake Lanier. My maternal grandfather, Joe Brown Williams, died in a car wreck on his way to the doctor. When they left home that day, they did not know it was their last. Most of us never think that today will be our last. Brad Paisley's song, "Last Time for Everything" is a great reminder that nothing lasts forever. You never know what today will bring. Live each day as if it were your last, because one day it will be.

When we search for and gain wisdom, we understand that our time on earth is short and precious. Wise people are grateful for their time here. Wise people also live their life from an eternal perspective. My belief, for example, is that there is life after death. Being raised in the Christian faith and my own spiritual journey have given me great respect for our Creator and our spiritual eternity. As we search for wisdom, each of us has to come to terms with eternity.

In simple terms, if there is no eternity, then it doesn't matter what you believe or how you live. When it's over, it's over. If there is eternal life, then there is meaning and purpose in all that we do. As we search for wisdom, meaning and purpose are what should motivate us.

MAXIM 7

Death is our greatest teacher.

Death is our greatest teacher. Don't fear death; learn from it. Embrace life—you never know which day will be your last. A wise person makes the most of the blessing that is today. The wise live life from an eternal perspective and are constantly searching for God's guidance on eternal life.

QUESTIONS TO PONDER:

1. Do you think you respect and understand death and its repercussions for life eternal?

2. If you fear death, can you think of ways to start living that would alleviate that fear?

3. What has death taught you about living?

PART THREE

Maxims from
FAMILY

MY GREATEST BLESSINGS AND MY greatest opportunities for growth as a person have come from being a father and a husband. Through the good times and the challenges, I have learned valuable lessons from my family. I wish we had taken more vacations together and made more family memories, but we have always been a family filled with love. My wife, Trisha, and my sons are the most important people in my life. I thank God every day for them.

Through our lives together I have learned the following maxims:

Patience, Grasshopper.

It's never too late.

Beware of acting in your own self-interest as opposed to the interests of others.

Always do your best.

Keep your word and be bold.

Be honorable.

PATIENCE, GRASSHOPPER

WE LEARN LIFE LESSONS IN ordinary ways. When we are wise enough to pay attention and get the message, our life gets better.

I learned a valuable lesson from my older son, Chess. He was moving to California from Nashville, and we had planned a cross-country road trip with a bucket list of places to see. One of our stops was the Grand Canyon. We drove to Williams, Arizona, where we spent the night and then caught a train to the Grand Canyon the next morning.

As always, I was up incredibly early. And as always, I was wound up tighter than a two-dollar watch. I was waiting for Chess to wake up so we could go to breakfast and get the day started. After about an hour, Chess got up and sensed my impatience. He looked at me and said, "Patience, Grasshopper." I originally heard the quote while watching the TV show *Kung Fu* in the 1970s, This was the first time I was moved by the power of the statement. And, for the first time in my life, I realized how impatient I had been my entire life. It hit me like a ton of bricks: I had spent my whole life thinking about something other than the blessing of the moment. I was in such a hurry to get to the next thing that I was missing the moment of the morning and the time I had with my son.

Those two words changed how I thought about life and set me on a path of noticing how impatient I was and how much better life is when you live in the moment. I also realized how much of my life I have missed by not being present. I had spent a great deal of my time wishing I were doing something else or thinking about what I should be doing next. I felt as if my life had been a blur.

But God works in strange ways. This was the perfect time to begin understanding the beauty of patience, and doing so allowed me to see that a day I might have previously experienced as intolerable due to its pace was in fact one of the best days of my life. As we arrived at the train, I saw a vintage locomotive with passenger cars like the ones you see in old Western movies. It was like stepping back in time. Once we boarded, I struggled to stay patient and in the moment. I kept my focus on the moment and let go of the thoughts of work issues back in Georgia that had constantly occupied my mind. When my thoughts would begin to race ahead, I would say to myself, "Patience, Grasshopper." As we rolled out of the station into the countryside, I saw that trees and prairie dogs lined the tracks. I noticed the people on board the train and the excitement in the eyes and faces of the young children. The train ride to the Grand Canyon was as slow as molasses, but I loved every minute of it. We met interesting people, and I noticed things I never would have seen had I not been truly present.

The greatest reward came when we arrived at the canyon. One of the ladies we met on the train was a career navy officer, and she was quite knowledgeable about the canyon. It was like having a professional instructor give us a crash course on how to approach it. She advised that when we got off the train, we shouldn't look at the canyon; we should keep our heads down and not look up until we got to the canyon's edge. Thank God I was patient and present enough to listen and follow her instructions. In that moment, when I finally allowed myself to look up, I saw the grandest, most beautiful, and most powerful sight of my life. There are no words to describe its grandeur. I was present in a way I had never been before in my life. It was all because of those words of wisdom from my son.

Be patient, Grasshopper. I have said these words to myself a thousand times since that morning. They continue to make my life so much more enjoyable and meaningful. Chess's words paid dividends after the birth of our first grandchild. I was present in the moment I first saw and held Grayson. I didn't let my mind race ahead to other concerns. I patiently watch him while he sleeps. I stop everything I am doing the moment he wakes up to be fully present. Patience and presence are two of life's greatest gifts. The wiser we become, the more aware and patient we become.

MAXIM 8
Patience, Grasshopper.

As you move through life, be patient, Grasshopper. Don't be so concerned with the life you wish you had. Be more concerned with the life you have, and all the blessings that surround you every minute of the day. It's *now* that matters—don't miss it. Take the time to change. When you apply this wisdom, life gets better.

QUESTIONS TO PONDER:

1. Right now, are you present in the moment? Give some thought to the people in your life. Are you truly *with* them when you are together?

2. Do you appreciate what they mean in your life, or have you been unconsciously short-changing them with your time or attention?

IT'S NEVER TOO LATE

AS A CHILD, MY SON, Chess, loved life. He always had things he wanted to do and places he wanted to go. When there was something he wanted to do, he would not let go of it. We could tell him no fifty times, and he would still ask for the fifty-first time. It would get to a point where it was too late—the movie was starting in thirty minutes or the store was closing at 6 p.m. I would say, "It's too late. We are not going to be able to do it." His answer was always, "It's never too late." He would not let go of the fact that we could still go. The reality was I made the choice not to go. There was—in most cases—enough time, but I chose not to use my time in the way Chess wanted. As I have gotten a little wiser, I am not as quick to say it's too late. Because of that change, life has given me some wonderful experiences that in the past I would have missed. For example, Chess had planned a trip to Florida the week of the Fourth of July. He was staying with his in-laws and visiting with friends who had a place on the beach. About two weeks out, he suggested that Trisha and I come along and bring Matt's family. It would have been easy to say it was too late. But taking my new approach, Trisha and I went to work finding a place to stay. Trisha booked us a two-bedroom condo on the beach not far from where Chess was staying. We had a wonderful time. Instead of making excuses for why we would never find a place to stay, we were blessed with our first family vacation in years!

Whenever I am faced with uncertainty about whether it's too late to do something, I always filter that uncertainty through Chess's words of wisdom: It's never too late. The most precious thing in life is our time. How we use that time will impact the quality of our life in ways we can't know. Be careful of saying it's too late, when what you should be doing is getting started. Getting started is one of our hardest challenges. Excuses for not getting started are a dime a dozen. In reality, if it is something we are meant to do, it's never too late. It's only too late if the Lord has called us home. If there is something you are called to do, get started.

An example for me is this book. It would have been easy to say it's too late to write, and I should have spent more time early in life putting my thoughts into words, or at sixty-three it's too late to get started—especially for a guy who has hardly written much more than his name. But instead, I focused on the wisdom of a child's enthusiasm for life—it's never too late.

MAXIM 9

It's never too late.

Life is always teaching us that it is short and time is precious. When we learn this lesson, we become wiser. Be careful of putting off what you are called to do. Is it really too late to take action, or are you making excuses? Find that childlike enthusiasm for life. It's never too late.

QUESTIONS TO PONDER:

1. What are the things you should be doing that you are not because you think it is too late?

2. Is it really too late?

BEWARE OF ACTING IN YOUR OWN SELF-INTEREST AS OPPOSED TO THE INTERESTS OF OTHERS

ONE OF THE HARDEST LESSONS I have had to learn in my life is to stop putting my own interest above the interest of others. Most of the time, I didn't even realize what I was doing. On many occasions, I have made decisions, big and small, and not even realized that I made the decision in my own best interest. In some cases, I even believed that I made the decision in someone else's best interests. I have been married for forty years, and my wife, Trisha, has always been remarkable about showing me my blind spots. Prior to retirement, most of what we did was arranged around my work schedule. I worked long hours and had a limited amount of free time. Trisha understood, and most of our activities were what I wanted to do. It seems I could find time for us to travel to a Georgia football game, but I could not find the time to take the family to the beach. I could pick a restaurant because it was easy to get to and had food I liked, but I never considered if it was where the others in the family wanted to eat. I thought if I liked it, they would like it. Now that I am no longer tied to my job, I realize how much of our time together was about me, when it should have been about us. Trisha has helped me to see this flaw, and I hope I am making ongoing improvements. At work and in sports, I had always put the team first, but in my personal life, I had shifted to a me-first attitude. Wise people know that everyone is prone to acting in their own self-interest. The more we understand and notice this, the better we see reality.

Seeing Reality and Being Aware

Wise people have the ability to see reality—not make reality fit their view of the world. Just watch two politicians debate an issue. They have their egos so wrapped up in defending their position that they say whatever they need to say to be right, all the while ignoring the possibility that their opponent might have a better idea. They are focused on their self-interest and the self-interest of their party; not on finding a better answer for the country. Have you ever noticed at your company that anytime there are management changes, people's questions tend to be about what the change means for them—not about how this will make the team better? To be a better leader, husband, father, teammate, or person, it is wise to understand when you or the person you are interacting with is serving his or her self-interest.

As I reflect on my life and the lives of those people I am close to, it seems whenever there was a discussion or a debate or an argument, both sides tended to make it about *being* right instead of discovering what *is* right. Now, after six decades of life lessons, I am more aware of this than ever before. Being able to recognize this tendency as it is happening is a trait of the wise. Our lives and the lives of those we care about get better when we make decisions that take into account not only our own self-interest but also the interest of others.

I grew up playing team sports and have always valued team first. Teams that do extraordinary things in sports and in business have story after story of individuals who put the team first. Jalen Hurts, the former quarterback at the University of Alabama, led the team to the national championship game his sophomore year. At halftime, he lost his starting position to a freshman. Alabama won the national championship. Jalen had every reason to transfer to another school. In two seasons, he had led Alabama to a record of twenty-six and two and was going into his junior season as the number-two quarterback on the depth chart. Jalen put his team's interest above his self-interest and stayed at Alabama. He continued to be a leader and a positive influence on the team. Most of the season he got limited playing time. But in the second half of the SEC championship against my beloved Georgia Bulldogs, he led Alabama to a come-from-behind victory and a chance to play for a national championship. Because Jalen put his team first, he and his teammates won an SEC championship. The world needs team-first players.

Be aware that individuals tend to act in their own self-interest: I certainly do under certain circumstance. But the wisest of individuals know that their decisions and actions affect their families, friends, sports teams, work teams, and other groups, and they consider not just their own self-interests but also the greater good of others.

MAXIM 10

Beware of acting in your own self-interest as opposed to the interests of others.

For our lives to have meaning, our actions must be bigger than ourselves. It's a tall order, but it's true.

QUESTIONS TO PONDER:

1. What steps or actions will you take today to put the interests of others above your own interests?

2. Who do you know that consistently puts the interest of the team above their own interest? Do you admire and want to follow that person?

3. What can you learn from their example? Is that person you?

ALWAYS DO YOUR BEST

I HAD ALWAYS LOVED WEARING the number one. I wore it when I was playing baseball and have always thought it was *the* number. When my younger son, Matt, was five years old, he played T-ball, and when it was time to decide who got which number, I encouraged him to request number one because it was my number.

He looked at me and said, "I want number two, because I am going to be twice as good as you." I thought that was such a powerful statement from a kid just starting to play the game. It says so much about the attitude we should have in life and who he was. He had no desire to be his dad; he wanted to be the best he could be. In his mind, he would have to be at least twice as good as I was to be the best he could be.

As I said in the prologue, the answers we are seeking are usually visible if we look in the obvious places. "Always do your best." How simple and how straightforward those words are. Matt's comments reminded me of how my mother always encouraged us to do our best. This often means separating yourself from the pack.

Separate Yourself from the Pack and Trust the Team

If you want to separate yourself from the pack, don't be a half-ass. Whether it is in business, your personal life, sports—you name it—do it right. Nothing gets under my skin more than leading a team with someone who is not pulling their weight. Seldom did I expect everyone to perform at the same level, but I always expected each team member to give their best. The people who give their best are the folks who earn the promotions and the opportunities to take on more responsibilities. It has been my experience that people who give their best are able to bring out the best in others. They are the folks people respect and will follow. I never saw a successful, happy, or wise half-ass. Every time you do something, commit to do it to the best of your ability and get better every time, every day. Life will reward you with its best. If you give your best, your team will respond with their best.

In my life experiences, when I gave my best (which, in some cases, was not enough), someone on the team would step up, and things worked out for the best. Some of my best business decisions involved letting go and trusting the talents of others. When I realized that a project needed more than I was providing, I would step back and hand the reins over to one of my teammates, and they would supply what was missing. For example, when we were working on a new sales presentation or a new business overview, I was good at pulling together the things that were important to the company and the sales force. But the magic happened when I got out of the way and turned the project over to our creative team. They were able to make our ideas into something special and memorable for the team. My teams always made me better than I was as an individual. Thank God for team. It's the greatest multiplier ever.

My experience has also taught me that if you are making important decisions regarding someone's life—a promotion, a termination, or a family member's challenges—it's important to get it right. People are counting on you. Sometimes your best isn't good enough. That's when a wise person looks up and seeks guidance from above. Many of my best decisions became clear when I was guided by a power I cannot explain but that I know exists.

MAXIM 11
Always do your best.

We should always do our best and always be committed to improving. Life gets better only when you get better. Your Creator knows when you're giving your best effort, and He will step in and do the rest. Nothing we do in life will be perfect, but the better our effort, the better the outcome.

QUESTIONS TO PONDER:

1. Identify at least one thing in your life that's important to you but where your effort is nowhere near your best.

2. What are some things you could do to improve?

3. Would the results of the changes be worth the effort?

KEEP YOUR WORD AND BE BOLD

"A MAN HAS TWO THINGS in life: his word and his manhood." This is a famous quote I heard from my son, Matt. I think he got it from some Al Pacino movie. Al and Matt's words were a little more graphic, and a little crude, so I used a modified version. Either way, there is wisdom in those words. As I go through life, it amazes me how few people today value being a person of their word. They say they will do something, and they never do it. I have been more aware of this since I retired, and I can't count the number of times people didn't show up when they said they would or didn't return my call. It's a matter of truth.

What does it say about a person who doesn't follow through on what they say they will do? One way to separate yourself from and be wiser than the pack is for your word to be your bond. A wise person does what he says. If circumstances change, follow up with those people who are impacted. It sounds obvious, but we should all be on guard and tell the truth and follow through on what we say. It seems like in today's society people will tell you a lie when it would be much easier to just tell the truth. Don't have people rearrange their precious time to meet with you and then not show up. Don't say you are coming to the meeting and not mean it. People lose respect for people who do not do what they say they will.

As a businessperson, have you ever purchased a software package or a business service only to find out the company overpromised and can't honor what they said they would? They said what they needed to say to make a sale. Wise people do what they say they will. When they tell you something you know you can count on them to honor their commitment.

Another universal truth we should give some thought to is that life favors the bold. We all need to be courageous. Most of us limit our lives and the lives of others we serve because we allow our lives to be controlled by fear. As I look back on my life, this is one area I would have doubled down on and hopefully will double down on in the future. While I have always believed I have more courage than most, I have limited my life because of fear. There have been countless times I have delayed doing something I knew I needed to do simply because I was uncomfortable doing it.

Have you ever put off calling a prospect because you were afraid they would say no? When you fret and worry over this feeling, it generally turns out to be much ado about nothing. When you reach the client, and they say no, you simply move on to the next client. Or, if the client says yes, then you have wasted all that emotional energy trying to get up the courage to call. All the while, the client was dying to hear from you. Franklin D. Roosevelt was right about there being nothing to fear but fear itself. Most of what we worry about never happens. A wise person should always be aware of the role fear plays in his or her life.

Fear Versus Stupidity

There is a big difference between fear and stupidity. Stupidity is jumping into the Grand Canyon and expecting to live. Fear is never going to the Grand Canyon because you are afraid of heights. We've got to be wise enough to find the right balance. Is your fear protecting you or limiting your life? Most things we fear are paper tigers that won't hurt anything but our pride. Beware of that nebulous feeling in your mind that you allow to control your life. We each have different fears and different degrees of fear. Sometimes, the things we fear most are the things we need to do—changing jobs, ending a toxic friendship, confronting a loved one. But often we don't do what we know we should do because we are paralyzed by fear. In these cases, we must find the courage to follow our heart and rely on faith in God to do the right thing. When in doubt, don't be reactive. Slow down and seek wisdom to do what God calls you to do. Then have the courage to do it.

I am no expert on fear and courage, but here are some thoughts to consider when you feel fear:

- Let it go.
- Use it to take action. Fear is energy.
- Feel the fear and do it anyway.

· Pray for wisdom and courage rather than stupidity. Don't jump out of a plane until you know how to do it. Sometimes fear is telling you you're not prepared—that more work is needed.

But most importantly, strive to be aware of fear and become more attuned to how it is affecting your life.

MAXIM 12
Keep your word and be bold.

Do what you say you are going to do. You are only as good as your word. Life favors people who keep their word and have the courage to take bold action when needed. These are traits of people who pursue wisdom.

QUESTIONS TO PONDER:

1. Who do you know who you can count on to do what they say?

2. Do you respect that person?

3. Are you a person who keeps their word?

4. Is there a situation in your life that needs bold action?

5. What will be required?

BE HONORABLE

I HAVE ALWAYS LOVED TO hunt quail. When I was a kid, I hunted just about anywhere in my hometown of Grayson, Georgia. Sometimes, someone would stop and question me. They would ask my name and whether I had permission to hunt on the land. I would answer with "Chess Britt" and "No, I do not have permission." Then they would ask if I was Walt Britt's grandson, and I would say, "Yes." At that point, they would say, "Go ahead and hunt." My grandfather was no longer living, but his impact on people remained.

It always perplexed me that those folks treated me special just because of who my grandfather was. Then one day I was eating at a small-town restaurant in nearby Lawrenceville, and a friend of my grandfather's was also eating there. We struck up a conversation. He said, "Your grandfather was an honorable man." It hit me in that moment—that's a pretty good way to be remembered fifteen or so years after your death.

My takeaway from that conversation was *Be an honorable man.* I have pondered what that means for my adult life. Now I don't know a lot about how my grandfather (I called him "Papaw.") earned that reputation. As a young boy, I had heard multiple stories about how, as a postmaster during World War II, he had opened the post office after hours so a parent could pick up a letter from a son. I had one man tell me that Papaw had a job measuring the amount of cotton farmers could plant during the Depression when the government paid subsidies to limit cotton production. The man said his family was in dire straits and had no money. They were running out of food, so my grandfather looked the other way on the small cotton overage they had planted. People treated me better than I deserved because of the respect they had for him.

There is a way to separate yourself and your life from other people and their lives: Be honorable; treat people like you would want to be treated—regardless of the circumstances. This may seem like a tall order, but it's well worth striving for.

MAXIM 13
Be an honorable person.

I can think of no better way to live your life or a better way to be remembered than as an honorable person. It might be wise to consider these words.

QUESTIONS TO PONDER:

1. Would most people say you're an honorable person?

2. If not, why?

3. Who are the people you can remember in your life who were honorable?

4. What effect did they have on you?

5. What about the people who were not honorable?

6. What effect did they have on you?

PART FOUR

Maxims from
FRIENDS

I HAVE BEEN BLESSED THROUGHOUT my life with friends who have made a positive impact on my philosophy. They have shared their wisdom in how they lived and in the conversations we have had. Thank God for the times I listened, learned, and grew from the lessons they were teaching.

My hope is that the following maxims will help you see the wisdom I have learned and put you in tune with the wisdom that life is teaching through your friends.

There is nothing good at the bottom of a bottle.

Nothing good comes from complaining.

Nothing good comes from feeling sorry for yourself.

No good deed goes unpunished.

Be humble, and guard against pride.

Be trustworthy.

It's going to be okay.

Count your blessings.

Make the most of your time with others.

THERE IS NOTHING GOOD AT THE BOTTOM OF A BOTTLE

I WAS HAVING A LIGHT conversation about drinking one day with my friend, Mike Adams. Mike, as he has done multiple times, said something that stuck with me from that moment forward. He had heard one of his relatives say, "There is nothing good at the bottom of a bottle." Now it's not my role to pass judgment on whether a person drinks or not, and if they do, how it might affect them or their life. My role is to give you things to think about. Like most things in life, it probably depends on the individual. As I have lived life and grown a little wiser, I offer these thoughts to consider:

Always have a respect for the power of the fruit of the vine. It can contribute to behavior you will regret. Those of us who have overindulged know what I am talking about.

Beware: Alcohol has the ability to make you think you are some-one you are not. You are never ten feet tall and bulletproof—no matter how much you drink.

If you engage in risky behavior for an extended period of time, the bear will eventually get on your back—and when it does, it is hell to get it off.

In today's social interactions, drinking is ingrained in every activity—dinner with friends, a sporting event, free time with a work colleague. Everyone is expected to drink. A wise person doesn't just follow the crowd; they are intentional about what they choose to do. I think we all know multiple people we love and care about who have a real problem with alcohol. You don't want to be the person encouraging them to drink. You might even want to be the person who chooses not to drink to support their sobriety. It's all a choice, so choose wisely. I saw a prominent individual give a speech about teenage drinking. Then he left the stage and went straight to the bar. I am not sure his actions were in alignment with his words. We should all be aware of the impact alcohol can have on our lives. It's important to make sure that we make choices that improve—not detract from—the quality of our lives and the lives of others. This maxim has been helpful in my life, and might be helpful as a guiding principle in yours.

MAXIM 14

There is nothing good at the bottom of a bottle.

Make wise choices that enhance your quality of life and the quality of life of those you love.

QUESTIONS TO PONDER:

1. Does this maxim have meaning for you or someone you love?

2. In what way?

3. If not, what is your guiding principle?

NOTHING GOOD COMES
FROM COMPLAINING

WHEN I WAS IN SIXTH grade, I was blessed to have a wonderful teacher, Mrs. Mary Frances Carter. She wanted to do more than just teach subject matter; she was always looking for an opportunity to teach character. One day in class, she had given us a bunch of math work to do. I started complaining. It seemed like too much, and I wondered out loud whether it was really necessary to do that much work.

To my surprise, Mrs. Carter stopped the entire class and read us a version of the Bible story of Joseph. Joseph is another Old Testament hero of mine because of Mrs. Carter. In Mrs. Carter's abbreviated version of the story, Joseph's brothers were jealous of him. He was the youngest son, born when his father was an old man. His father loved him dearly and treated him differently than his other sons. When Joseph was a teen, his father gave him a beautiful, colorful, long-sleeved robe, and the brothers' jealousy grew to hatred. His brothers treated him with disdain, but Joseph never complained. When the opportunity presented itself, his brothers sold him as a slave to travelers from another country who were going to Egypt. Believing they would never see him again; they soaked his robe in animal blood and convinced their father he had been killed by a wild animal.

The travelers ultimately sold him as a slave to an Egyptian officer of the Pharaoh. In Mrs. Carter's story, he never complained but made the most of his circumstances. Even when he was falsely accused of something he did not do and put in prison, he never complained. When it was all said and done, he became the second-most powerful person in Egypt next to the Pharaoh and was able to prevent his family from starving to death during a prolonged famine. The moral at the end of Mrs. Carter's story was, "Never complain; make the most of your circumstances, and what you think is bad might turn out be a blessing." So, I stopped complaining, sucked it up, and did the math assignment.

Thank God I listened to what she said. It impacted me for the rest of my life. Anytime someone reminds me that I am complaining, or if I catch myself, I think of Mrs. Carter's wise words about how nothing good comes from complaining. If you make the most of your circumstances like Joseph, the thing you are complaining about could be a blessing in disguise. You never know if what's happening to you in any given situation is good or bad—only time will tell. Often the most important thing is not what's actually happening; it's how you react to it. Most of my experiences in life that I thought were disasters turned out to be blessings.

When I was young, I loved being outside. I spent my time hunting, fishing, and playing sports. Throughout high school and college, I had summer jobs outdoors. I labored for a brick mason crew, built road bridges, and worked for a general contractor building houses. In college, my major was accounting. The most important thing I learned in college was that I did not want to be an accountant. So, I got my real estate license. After three days in a real estate office, being inside was driving me crazy. I went back to construction work. To make a long story short, a few years later I was married with a kid on the way, and not making any money. Interest rates were through the roof, and residential construction had tanked.

I got a call from my best friend Rick Mathis who had started working for a new company that had an entry-level position available. He believed there would be a lot of opportunities to grow with the company. I didn't want to take a job working inside. I thought I would be miserable, but I needed a job. It turned out to be the best thing that could have happened. At one of the first talks I heard the founder, Art Williams, give, he said, "I wanted to build a company like you build a football team."

I knew at that moment this was where I wanted to be. Fast forward thirty-six years. I've had an amazing experience. I was blessed to have worked with great people, great leaders, and great friends. I loved what I did. Rick was right. There was opportunity to grow. I started in a clerical position and ended up as the chief marketing officer. Not bad for a guy who at the start did not even want to walk in the door. I followed Mrs. Carter's advice and made the most of my circumstances. I did everything I was asked to do and more. I did not spend my time complaining but stayed focused on growing as a leader and doing whatever I could to help the company win. If I had spent my time complaining about starting at the bottom and being worth more than I was getting paid, things would have turned out much differently. I doubt I would be financially independent with the freedom to write this book and spend more time with my family than at any point in my adult life.

The Primerica leadership had a remarkable influence on my growth as a leader and as a human being. I'm blessed beyond words for Rick's phone call, and to have been a part of a phenomenal company. I know of no wise person who constantly complains about what's happening in their life, and I know of no complainers about whom people say, "That's someone I admire, respect, and want to be around." I am thankful for Mrs. Carter's wisdom to stop class, not to embarrass me, but to teach me a life lesson. Life is so much better when you make the most of your circumstances. Just writing this reminds me of how much room there is for me to improve.

MAXIM 15
Nothing good comes from complaining.

Mrs. Carter, you were right: Nothing good comes from complaining.

QUESTIONS TO PONDER:

1. Instead of complaining about today's challenges, how else can you react to move yourself forward in a positive way?

2. Can you distinguish between complaining and standing up for what you believe is right?

3. How or when did complaining improve or hurt your quality of life?

NOTHING GOOD COMES FROM FEELING SORRY FOR YOURSELF

SPORTS HAVE ALWAYS BEEN A big part of my life. I grew up playing them year-round. Today, I love being at a live sporting event at the University of Georgia or at one of the games of the high school team my son coaches. I'd like to share a great piece of wisdom I learned from my high school football coach, Bobby Johnson. In the early seventies, football was still old school. To prevent cramps we ran more wind sprints in practice. The worse the weather, the better the practice. There was no such thing as too hot or too cold. It all just made you tougher and more game ready. Our first practice of the year was the worst. It was designed to test our mettle to see who was committed and who would quit. We would end practice by running wind sprints until nobody had any gas left in the tank. To play, you had to be willing to pay a price and commit to the toughness of practice. If you didn't, you didn't come back to practice the next day.

During my first high school practice of the regulation season, I had the flu but didn't know it. I thought I was just nervous.

So, I practiced that day but felt like crap. We ended practice with wind sprints that were designed to push you to your limits. I thought I was dying, and I probably was. I never said anything about it to anyone during practice because I did not want to seem weak. The thing that got me through that practice was Coach Johnson saying, "Don't feel sorry for yourself. The only person who will feel sorry for you is your momma, and she isn't here." Thank goodness Coach realized after practice that I had the flu, and he understood I needed some time to get well.

But in life when things have gotten hard and I've begun to feel sorry for myself, I think about what Coach said. There's a lot of truth and wisdom in those words. Most of the time people are focused on themselves, and they have little concern for how you feel anyway. They certainly are not concerned with you feeling sorry for yourself.

No Pity Parties

Self-pity will take you nowhere but down. Throughout my life, remembering these words has helped me put things into perspective. At work, when the workload demanded an exceptional effort—which was pretty much most of the time—if I sensed self-pity in my words or actions or in those on the team, I would put things in perspective. What I was doing wasn't really work, I told myself. This was nothing compared to the work I did in construction. In fact, compared to what I used to do, I haven't really had to work a day of my life since starting with Primerica.

I was blessed to be doing what I was doing—and besides, nobody was going to feel sorry for me but my momma, and she wasn't here. When teammates began to feel some self-pity, the Coach Johnson maxim helped them realize that even if a particular task were demanding, complaining wasn't going to make things better. Self-pity benefits no one—especially not you. A wise man will be on guard against it. It will hit, and when it does, remember that nobody is feeling sorry for you. Don't look down, look up. The good Lord's strength and energy is a better answer than self-pity.

MAXIM 16
Nothing good comes from feeling sorry for yourself.

Avoid self-pity and complaining. Wise people figure out that that these are not traits of happy, successful people. While empathy for others is a positive emotion, most people really don't care about or want to hear about you feeling sorry for yourself. To be an attractive person, be positive and excited about life regardless of the temporary circumstances.

QUESTIONS TO PONDER:

1. Does self-pity make you feel better or worse?

2. What are the consequences of spending time feeling sorry for yourself?

3. How do you feel when you find yourself with someone who is consumed by self-pity?

NO GOOD DEED GOES
UNPUNISHED

MY GOOD FRIEND, SOUTHERN PHILOSOPHER, storyteller, and former Primerica co-CEO, John Addison, came by my office one afternoon. He sat down and said, "Always remember, no good deed goes unpunished." I had heard the words but never really thought about what they meant.

He had just met with one of our top sales force leaders who, over the years, he had developed a great friendship and business relationship with. Now John had helped this guy multiple times, having even gone to bat to save his career at one point. Given everything John had done for him, he was making plans to start a business venture that he should have known could never coexist with our business. The way he handled the matter was not what you would have expected from a friend and trusted business partner.

John is not one to hold a grudge, so he read the guy the riot act and then helped him get out of the mess he had created.

How could someone you had helped multiple times do something with no consideration of your friendship or loyalty to them? Hard to believe, but true.

The moral of this story is that there will be times when you do the right thing and people will have no appreciation for what you did to help them. So always do the good deed, but don't be surprised by the actions of those you help.

Regardless, Do the Right Thing

There are some who will appreciate what you have done, and they will pay you back tenfold. Others will disrespect you. Regardless, do the right thing. You are responsible for your actions. Life will teach you that your actions won't always be appreciated. There will be times when even friends and family will surprise you with a lack of appreciation. A wise person will do the good deed with no concerns for how others should act.

Life is full of contradictions. The other day, Trisha and I were eating at a Japanese restaurant where they cook at the table for the group. There was a young couple sitting beside us whose premature baby had been in the neonatal intensive care unit for an extended period of time. They had the weight of the world on their shoulders and had come to the restaurant to take a little time to enjoy a meal away from work and the hospital.

Trisha and I were moved by their circumstances and wanted to do a little something to help lighten their load. So, we offered to buy their meal. They refused at first but understood it was important to us, so they finally agreed.

We had walked to the restaurant, but when Trisha and I

left it was pouring rain, so we sat on a bench under an awning trying to decide whether to leave and get soaked or wait it out. The wait would have been hours.

To our surprise, the young couple we had treated to a meal saw us from the road. They turned around, came back to the restaurant, and offered us a ride home. Of course, we accepted. This couple we did not know went out of their way to repay our small favor.

As we search for wisdom, what matters is our character. If it is the right thing, do the good deed. Expect nothing in return. If you are on the receiving end of a good deed, be like the young couple and show your appreciation.

MAXIM 17
No good deed goes unpunished.

A wise person will do the good deed and expect nothing in return. They will not be surprised if they are punished or rewarded. If they are blessed by someone else's good deed, they will react like the young couple with appreciation rather than the indignation of the sales leader.

QUESTIONS TO PONDER:

1. What was your most recent good deed?

2. How did the person you helped react?

3. What is the most recent good deed someone did for you?

4. How did you react?

5. Have you ever done a good deed because it was the right thing to do with no regard for how the other person would react?

6. What was the good deed?

BE HUMBLE,
AND GUARD AGAINST PRIDE

IT HAS BEEN MY EXPERIENCE in life that when you begin to think you know more than you actually do, or if you become cocky or judgmental, bad things are bound to happen. The saying, "Pride comes before a fall" seems to be true. As I have lived and studied life, I have come to believe that when pride and conceit take hold of your life, you will screw things up.

I worked with a lady named Frances early in my career. I was in my late twenties and did not really know much about anything. She was a wonderful person whom I grew to love dearly, but she always did things her way. She wasn't the best at taking directions, to put it mildly. Frances was not keen on listening to some kid's ideas on how to improve her area.

Me being a little hardheaded myself, we had some epic confrontations, which usually resulted in her not changing a darn thing. My hat's off to Frances. Working with her was a great education. She challenged me, and I learned more about how to deal with people than at any other period in my career. One of her favorite sayings when she was talking about me, or one of my peers, was, "The young man has shit in his neck, and it needs to be stomped out." That's a more graphic way to say pride comes before the fall.

Frances's words have stuck with me as words of wisdom. Whenever I start to feel my oats, life puts me in my place.

Be Humble and Kind

Tim McGraw wrote a song for his daughters that had a great line about always being humble and kind. The wisest people I have met or studied were humble and kind. Those who become consumed by pride eventually run things into the ditch. Don't be one of those people. Be aware and look out for those situations when you have crap in your neck and you are full of yourself. Realize that life is warning you that you are one step closer to disaster. Life will humble you, and it won't stop until you learn the lesson. Thank God for Frances who made me aware early in my life of the dangers of being full of crap.

Easier Said Than Done

Now being aware and actually living by the principle are two different things. But for me, being aware is the beginning of change. As you strive to become wiser, you should study pride and humility and be aware at any moment in life of where you are.

I have been blessed to be around some really strong, powerful leaders. When they were in the zone and doing wonderful things for the people they were leading, they had their egos in check. But once their ego and pride controlled their decisions, they ran things into the ditch. Study powerful people and you'll see that when things go badly, it's usually because they became full of crap. They thought they knew more than they did. They began to believe they were invincible, and they started doing dumb stuff.

The wise, powerful leaders I have been exposed to in life were great at keeping their egos in check and were self-actualized enough to know when they were full of themselves.

MAXIM 18
Be humble, and guard against pride.

In your search for wisdom, strive to be humble and kind. Know when you have crap in your neck that needs to be stomped out. Never forget that pride cometh before a fall. This is true in the big and the little decisions of life.

QUESTIONS TO PONDER:

1. Do you believe pride cometh before the fall?

2. If so, what's your plan to keep pride in check?

3. Can you think of times in your life or in the lives of others you know where pride and lack of humility led to a bad outcome?

4. Did you learn from it and change the course of your life?

BE TRUSTWORTHY

I'D LIKE TO SHARE A case study in trust. When I was in the fifth grade, my lifelong best friend, Rick Mathis, was the teacher's pet. Rick was one of the best students in class and overall a great guy. Mr. Garrett, our teacher, thought Rick hung the moon. Every day after lunch, Mr. Garrett would go to the principal's office where he took about thirty minutes to smoke a cigarette and relax. Now the rule was that we were to use those thirty minutes for study hall. Rick was left in charge. There was to be no talking or misbehaving. Rick's job was to take names of anyone who violated the rule. But what was supposed to be study hall turned into a fifth-grade version of *Animal House*—every day.

Now to understand the story, you need to realize that Mr. Garrett was the ultimate disciplinarian. You just did *not* misbehave in his class. If you did, he was the best at correcting your behavior by having you write out the names of all the states and their capitals. Or he would spank your tail with a paddle. Nobody messed with Mr. Garrett.

So, no one in the school expected us to do anything but follow Mr. Garrett's instructions. When he left the class, the room turned into a scene of everyone doing whatever they wanted to do: talking, running around, playing games, and generally having a great time for thirty minutes. Rick, being a fun-loving guy, was the ringleader, and he had more fun than anybody.

But for this to continue, it was understood that Rick was going to turn in two or three names to Mr. Garrett from time to time. You never knew if it was your turn in the barrel; anyone was fair game, even Rick's best friend. It was a fifth grader's high-stakes poker game. For the fun to keep going, we knew someone had to get in trouble. Mr. Garrett trusted the class, and we trusted each other not to tell what was going on. We took advantage of Mr. Garrett's trust and trusted each other for the wrong reasons. Thank goodness, he never questioned us about what was going on—and no real harm was ever done. We took our punishment, and the fun continued.

Today, I love to tell this story around Rick and give him a hard time about being the teacher's pet and tattling on his best friend. And this is my version of what happened; Rick might tell a different version, but the point is that this story allows us to discuss the difference between trust and deception.

The Thing about Trust

People you can truly trust seem to be the rarest of all. As we strive to become wiser, we should ask ourselves whether we can be trusted. When people can trust you and you can trust them, life gets better. When we violate trust, life becomes chaotic and full of betrayal.

Our lives are built on trusting more people today than at any point in human history. Think for a minute about all the people you have to trust to get on an airplane, from the worker in the maintenance facility to the supplier of parts to the mechanic—the pilot, the air traffic controller—the list goes on. If any one of those individuals chose to violate the trust placed in them, then that plane ride could become a disaster.

Our world needs trustworthy people. Whenever I need help, I look for someone I can trust. Whether it's financial advice, someone to work on my house, repair my car, teach or coach my kids—you name it—one of my highest priorities is trust. You can separate yourself from others by working to be a person whom others can trust in all circumstances. As a guy who grew up playing sports, I realized that, to be successful, everybody on the team had to trust each other to do their job. We had to trust that when someone was struggling, someone else would pick up the slack.

Not only do we need to be a person who can be trusted; we need to build trustworthy teams. In my work career, the characteristic I respected most in people I worked with was trustworthiness. Could they be trusted to do the right thing? I had one rule for people who worked for me: no surprises. I needed to trust that if something in our company was going well or badly, my people would let me know about it. Nothing tripped my switch more than to find out we had a problem and the leader had not updated me on what was happening. In return,

I gave them tremendous flexibility in how they accomplished team goals.

It was also important to me to treat my leadership like I wanted to be treated. So I placed a high level of importance on not letting them be surprised by anything of significance that was happening in my areas of responsibility. A great way to earn trust is to avoid having someone hear about an issue from someone other than you. They might not like what you tell them, but it's a lot better than them hearing it from a peer or their leader. There is astonishing power in trust and tremendous damage in its betrayal. My career was continually influenced by this idea.

Our company's business model is built on a partnership with our sales force. The most significant factor in our successes is building relationships based on trust. Anytime I had a conversation or business dealing with a member of our sales force, it was important to me to not mislead them. I wanted them to trust what I said. I never wanted them to be deceived by my words or actions. We may have disagreed, or they may have disliked my decisions or the company's decisions, but they knew they could trust me to tell them the truth. Nothing destroys a leader or a company's credibility faster than a lie. The wise leaders I have dealt with were trustworthy.

Here's the thing about trust: you can spend a lifetime building it. You must value it and understand that one untrustworthy decision could permanently destroy a lifetime of work. History is littered with examples of this. Think about Dan Rather, who was the face and voice of CBS News. He was considered by many to be the most trusted news anchor in America. He made one misleading statement and lost a lifetime of credibility and one of the most prestigious jobs in America. Don't miss this point. The world needs individuals, teams, companies, and other organizations that value trust. This starts with individuals who are worthy of our trust.

MAXIM 19
Be trustworthy.

We must all be aware of the importance and power of honesty. Be the wisest and rarest of people; be the person that others trust. And always be on guard against the perils of betraying the trust of others. If we all improve in this area, our lives and the lives of others improve exponentially.

QUESTIONS TO PONDER:

1. Do you believe it's important to be a person others can trust?

2. If so, why?

3. Name the three people you trust the most.

4. Are there things you can learn from their example?

5. What would others say about you if I asked them if you could be trusted?

IT'S GOING TO BE OKAY

MY DAD AND MOM GAVE us hope that regardless of what was happening around us, everything was going to be okay. They never taught us that things were going to be easy, or that they were going to be exactly what we wanted—just that they would be okay. That belief has played out in my life, and it seems to me that wise people have the ability to take the trials and challenges of life and turn them into meaningful experiences that end up helping them grow as people.

This makes me think of Mary Durham Cawley, another wonderful person I was blessed to work with in my career. Mary had an uncanny ability to help you know—regardless of the circumstances—that everything was going to be okay. I always respected her for her faith and lack of doubt. She ran our meetings and conventions group at my former company, and if you have ever been involved in running large meetings, you know they are full of uncertainty.

During the time Mary and I worked together, not only were

we doing crazy meetings, we were doing them under the leadership of what seemed to us to be an alien life form. Our company had always had an entrepreneurial spirit and held its sales force in the highest regard. By the time Mary started reporting to me, our company had been sold to a big corporation, which introduced a great many challenges. The focus of the parent company was not always aligned with how our company had been built, and this created all sorts of choppy waters that we had to navigate.

The meetings area was a new responsibility for me; I had no experience in it, while Mary was a true pro at what she did. During this time, we had corporate executives trying to change the company, while others were holding true to the values that had made us successful. This made it almost impossible to find the right balance and do what was in our company's best interest.

Through these crazy times, I learned from Mary that things were going to be okay; you just had to have faith and trust that the good Lord had a way of getting things to the right spot. We worked hard and always tried to do the right thing, striking a balance between the old and new business philosophies. Through it all, we ultimately had success. While I was filled with doubt from my lack of experience and faith, Mary was the ultimate in believing that things would be okay.

In 2003, Mary gave me a Bible for my birthday, and one of the scriptures she noted was James 1:2–8:

Profiting from Trials

My brethren, count it all joy when you fall into various trials, knowing that testing of your faith produces patience. But let patience have its perfect work, that you may be perfect and complete, lacking nothing. If any of you lack wisdom, let him ask of God, who gives to all liberally and without reproach, and it will be given to him. But let him ask in faith, with no doubting, for he who doubts is like a wave of the sea driven and tossed by the wind. For let not that man suppose that he will receive anything from the Lord, he is a double-minded man, unstable in all his ways.

Now this is pretty deep—you might need to read it multiple times over multiple days. But the words are words of wisdom and power. As best I can tell, Jesus's life and teachings were the best there have ever been. I will talk about this more later in the book. It seems nobody would have known Jesus better than his brother James. So to me, these words are words from the Master of wisdom and truth.

Life is a crapshoot. You never know what tomorrow holds. It's faith, not doubt, that makes life a rewarding and meaningful adventure. Our lives are filled with trials and uncertainty. It's in these life trials that we grow in wisdom and in spirit. The wise know that ultimately everything is going to be okay. They work every day to tap into the power of faith over doubt. John Lennon of the Beatles is credited with saying, "Everything will be okay in the end. And if it is not okay, it's not the end." The belief that it's going to be okay is a powerful guide when dealing with uncertainty.

MAXIM 20
It's going to be okay.

As you seek wisdom in your life, consider the wisdom in James 1:2–8. Become aware of the power of faith in your Creator versus living a life of doubt, fear, and worry about tomorrow. The wise know if they do the right thing, ultimately, everything will be okay.

QUESTIONS TO PONDER:

1. When you face trials and uncertainty in your life, what role does doubt play?

2. What role does faith play?

3. Which one has given you the most energy to deal with your challenges?

4. Do you believe everything will ultimately be okay?

5. Why do you believe that?

COUNT YOUR BLESSINGS

MY NEXT-DOOR NEIGHBOR, BILL LONGINO, made a toast at his daughter's wedding, quoting one of his father's favorite sayings. The words focus on what blesses us in life. If we have the basic necessities, then we have much to be thankful for:

> "May you always ride an easy walking horse, sleep beneath a rain-tight roof, and eat high on the hog all the days of your life."

To have transportation, a roof over your head, and something good to eat means you are blessed with more than the majority of people on earth. To grow as a person and to grow in wisdom, I believe we need to always remind ourselves of the blessings we have and to give thanks for those blessings. For most of us who have the basics, everything else is abundance. Life is so much better when you focus on what you have as opposed to what you don't have.

Most of us are blessed with the necessities of life. But we never consider how miraculous these blessings are, or what it took for us to have them. Whenever I question if there are miracles in life, all I have to do is look around and count my blessings.

I am sitting here watching a beautiful, one-of-a-kind sunrise and drinking a hot cup of coffee. It's beyond my imagination how that sunrise happens every day. No other sunrise will ever be like this one. Since the beginning, we have been blessed with the warmth and beauty of the sun. But let's simplify it and consider how miraculous it is to have that hot cup of coffee, and how blessed I am that it ever made its way to me. It took sunshine, seed, water, and dirt. It took a farmer to plant, care for, and harvest the bean. Somehow it got processed, packaged, and transported to my house. Then I had the coffeemaker, the cup, the water, the electricity—I think you get the picture. Just for me to have the pleasure of enjoying that cup of coffee, thousands, if not millions of things had to come together. That's a miracle.

I heard a wise man say that the ability to live a life of gratitude is the beginning of abundance. Makes sense to me. As best I can tell, it's where we should all start if our goal is to have life and have it abundantly. Having an attitude of gratitude puts everything else in perspective.

We go through life focused on what we want as opposed to what we have. Like me, most folks reading this book likely go through life putting pressure on themselves to achieve more, have more, be more. When we do that, we lose sight of what we have.

Real Pressure

I saw Shaquille O'Neal, the former superstar NBA player, give a TV interview and talk about the things he learned from his dad. Shaq recalled one game during his professional basketball career when he didn't play very well. After the game, he got a call from his dad. His dad said, "Son, come home. We need to talk." Shaq did what his dad asked, got on a private plane, and went home.

His dad asked him if he had let pressure get to him during the game. Shaq thought about it and said, "Yes, I did."

His dad, being wise, said, "Son, let's get in the car." They rode through areas of the city where people had real pressures. He told Shaq, "What you felt last night was not pressure. Pressure is not knowing where your next meal is coming from." His dad, through his wisdom, helped his son put things in perspective. He was blessed more than most people could even imagine.

MAXIM 21
Count your blessings.

Always count your blessings. They are, for most of us, greater than we ever imagined. When you find yourself grateful, you tend to have the wisdom to appropriately deal with life's blessings and challenges. When we are focused on what we don't have, we tend to live life below our peak performance. We beat ourselves up and underperform. Remember, counting your blessings is the beginning of abundance.

QUESTIONS TO PONDER:

1. Do you have transportation, a place to live, and something to eat?

2. Are you wise enough to be thankful for these miraculous blessings?

3. How else has life blessed you?

4. How much of your time is spent counting your blessings versus worrying about what you don't have?

5. How could you work on changing this?

MAKE THE MOST
OF YOUR TIME WITH OTHERS

YESTERDAY, I ATTENDED THE FUNERAL of a friend and teammate from work, David Wade. David was a true hero at our company. Through his hard work and dedication, we had a state-of-the-art data center and technology infrastructure. Funerals, as I said earlier, always seem to leave me a little wiser and with a better understanding of life. David's life taught lessons in dedication, teamwork, commitment, and loving people. But above and beyond everything to do with David's work accolades, I most remember him for a day we spent in Washington, D.C.

We had a meeting planned with one of the companies we do business with. David convinced me that we should go up a day early and see some sights in D.C. This was a little out of character for me at that time in my career, since things were so busy that I never felt I had a day to waste. But David convinced me it would be worth it. He had two main things on his list that we had to see: National Gallery of Art and the newly completed Vietnam Veterans Memorial Wall.

The last thing I would have ever considered visiting was an art museum, but it seemed to be important to David, so I agreed to go. Little did I know how much David knew about art. As we walked through the museum, it was as if I had my own curator as a personal guide. Through David's words and enthusiasm, I felt a whole new appreciation for the amazing paintings. Through David's words, they all had a story—the time period when they were painted, the artist, the meaning of the work, the value of the art. He helped me, for the first time in my life, to see the beauty and awe of these magnificent works. From that day forward, anytime I've seen a painting, I've thought of David's lesson on art, and I see and appreciate things that I would have never appreciated if not for David.

The other moment we shared together that impacted us both very deeply was visiting the Vietnam Veterans Memorial Wall. We were there on Mother's Day. Hundreds of mothers were coming to the wall and lighting candles and leaving letters in memory of their sons and daughters who were killed in the war. It was one of the most moving days of our lives. David picked up one letter and read it aloud. What I expected to hear was a mother's message to a fallen soldier. But it was a message of a mother recalling her eighteen-year-old son. How she would always remember him as the young man she saw leave one day for war and never come back.

Being a man whose father had fought in two wars, I was touched very deeply by David's reading of a mother's precious last memories of her son. It made the wall more than a memorial; it was a living memory of the lives of our fallen soldiers and the sacrifices made by them and their families.

As our careers grew and we both took on more responsibility, David and I did not spend as much work time or travel time together. But that day in D.C. bonded our friendship and respect for a lifetime. The last few years of my career, we had quarterly officers' meetings, and it seemed that at most meetings David and I sat together in the front row—and more times than one we talked about our day in D.C. What a wonderful day it was. It was an incredible memory that I was able to share with a truly unique and wonderful human being and friend.

Don't Miss the Opportunity to Make Lasting Memories

I tell this story to honor David, but more than that, I tell it to say that David impacted my life on that day in a truly unique way that shaped me for the rest of my life. As we search for wisdom and meaning in our lives, know that our daily actions and our time with friends and acquaintances hold one of the most important keys to having life and having it in abundance. Don't miss the opportunity to make lasting memories with the people you share your life with. *David, the next time we share our thoughts about our day together will be the best. Thanks for your life and the impact you had on me and so many others.*

MAXIM 22

Make the most of your time with others.

Every day matters; you never know what impact you will make on those you spend time with. Be wise and realize that wise people love others and appreciate the time they spend together. It doesn't matter whether it's five minutes or fifty years. Love others. Love life. It's love that will complete you and lead you on your search for wisdom and spiritual fulfillment.

QUESTIONS TO PONDER:

1. If your friends reflected on your time together, what lasting memories would they talk about?

2. Would those memories be meaningful?

3. When was the last time you made a lasting memory with a friend? Is there an opportunity to do it today?

PART FIVE

Maxims from
ACQUAINTANCES

SOME OF MY LIFE'S GREATEST lessons have come from people I never knew well enough to call my friends. But because our paths crossed, my life got better. Always be open to having a conversation. You can learn from everyone. They might turn out to be one of your greatest teachers. Maxims from some of my acquaintances include the following:

Beware of "Woe is me."

Nature puts life in perspective.

Feed and water the mules.

Never have a bad day.

BEWARE OF "WOE IS ME"

HAVE YOU EVER HAD ONE of those days when you are down on life? Your personal life, your work life? You just feel like you are at an all-time low. The more you focus on how you feel, the worse you feel. I had one of those days in a hotel room in Dallas, Texas. I was driving myself crazy with my "Woe is me" thinking. It hit me that I needed to get some fresh air and stop thinking about me. As I walked by a restaurant, I encountered a man who asked if I would buy him lunch. In that moment, it felt like we were meant to spend some time together. I had given several people money to get something to eat, but I had never asked anyone to join me for lunch. He seemed to be about my age, and based on his clothes, he appeared to be down on his luck. We had lunch together, and he told me his story.

Two months earlier, he was drinking with some friends after work in Dallas. A fight broke out, and he got arrested and put on probation. He lost his job because he didn't show up for work while he was in jail. He couldn't leave Dallas, and all his family was in St. Louis. He had no support system and couldn't find and keep a job because of his legal challenges. If he left Dallas and went home to St. Louis, he would go to jail for a probation violation. He was caught in our legal system. He had run out of money and was staying in a shelter. His life had spiraled down to a point where he was doing what he could to survive until his probation was up and he could go home. That lunch helped put my life in perspective. The man was a good soul who had made a mistake and was paying the price for his mistake. He taught me two lessons: Things could always be worse than they are, and when you are focused on yourself rather than others, life is a struggle.

MAXIM 23
Beware of "Woe is me."

Thank God for that lunch and the lesson learned from that gentleman. Wisdom calls us to be grateful for our blessings. By helping others, we help ourselves. Anytime you are unhappy and struggling in life, my bet is that you are focused on "Woe is me" as opposed to thinking of others. Change your focus and change your life. There is a God, and it is not you.

QUESTIONS TO PONDER:

1. When was the last time you were focusing on "Woe is me"?

2. Were things really as bad as they seemed?

3. How did you move forward?

4. How should you have moved forward?

NATURE PUTS LIFE IN PERSPECTIVE

SEVERAL YEARS AGO, MY FRIEND Ed Snell and I were quail hunting in Texas. We stayed in a hunting lodge along with the Robertson family of *Duck Dynasty* fame. They were filming a duck hunt. It was before the show was on TV, so at that time I didn't know who they were. They were characters, but the real character was our hunting guide. He is a guy who woke up one morning, told his wife he was going to Wal-Mart, and then went to the hunting camp and never went home. That's probably not the wisest way to end a marriage.

On the first day of our hunt, he taught me a valuable lesson. Now I love being in Texas, but most of the land we hunted all looked the same. It was filled with shinnery bushes and prairie grass, which I think are beautiful—especially if they support a healthy quail population. It was a sunny, gorgeous morning with that constant Texas wind. We walked up on one of the most picturesque pieces of land I had ever seen in Texas. Our guide was the first to realize what a magnificent sight it was. It had rolling hills and a beautiful pond. It was a sight to behold. As we were soaking in the moment, I started talking about building a house on a spot on the other side of the pond and talking about other changes I would make to the property. Our guide looked at me and said, "That land is perfect just like it is. The last thing it needs is a house on it."

That was one of the first times in my life I realized just how perfect God's creation is. I saw a beautiful creation—not something to change to my liking. There was clarity in those moments we rested on that spot. I felt an amazing calm and connection to nature. A wise person is in tune with nature and sees and feels its beauty. When life is spinning out of control and you need perspective, take a walk, watch the sunrise, sit on your back porch and soak up the beauty God has placed all around us.

Be Smarter Than Me

Be smarter than me, and don't spend your time wanting to change nature, wishing the temperature was warmer, or the grass was greener. Just realize how blessed you are to see that one-of-a-kind sunrise. Love what you are experiencing; not what you wish you were experiencing. Make life stop spinning out of control, be present in the moment, and get perspective. Once you do this, whatever is bothering you, causing you to be stressed, anxious, fearful, or angry will be soaked in positive emotions.

I don't know why it is like this. I just know that when we are in tune and in touch with nature, we get perspective. Problems and challenges seem to get smaller. Your ego is put in check, and you realize how small your issues are in comparison to the magnificence of God's creations. You realize nothing you can do or have done will ruin life's magnificence. Your perspective on life and your direction in life become clear, and you are energized to tackle today's challenges.

MAXIM 24
Nature puts life in perspective.

When a wise person needs perspective on life, they should take time to experience God's magnificent creation. Be present and experience the awesome beauty of Mother Nature. It will change your perspective and energize your day.

QUESTIONS TO PONDER:

1. What will you do today to gain perspective on your life?

2. Can you think about a time when being in nature caused you to let go and get perspective? What is your favorite thing in Mother Nature?

3. Is it the beach?

4. The sunrise?

5. When was the last time you truly soaked it in?

6. Did it make a positive impact on what you were feeling and thinking?

FEED AND WATER THE MULES

WHEN I WAS A KID, I heard one of my dad's friends tell a story. He said when he was a boy, he walked up on a sharecropper who was resting with his mules under a shade tree. The overseer who owned the property was also there and was steaming mad that the man did not have the mules out in the field working. The overseer was on the verge of attacking the sharecropper, when the sharecropper looked at the overseer and said, "If you want to make crops, you have to feed and water the mules." That saying stuck with me.

It's a great story with insights on farm life in rural Georgia when my dad was growing up. As a kid, I loved to hear him talk about life on the farm—the hard work involved and the challenges of plowing with a mule. How important it was to have a healthy mule and how difficult it was to get a stubborn mule to plow a straight row. After I heard the story, I would ask myself who was right. How did you know when the mules needed rest? Was the sharecropper being smart or lazy? Then

I turned the question on myself. When I rested, was it because I needed the rest, or was I just being lazy? At a young age, I concluded that if you wanted to make a crop, you'd better feed and water the mules.

Throughout my working career, there were two things you could count on: I was a hard worker, and I always ate lunch thanks to the wisdom I learned from a sharecropper I never knew. But the message in the sharecropper's words means more to me than the importance of eating and resting. They speak to the wisdom of not living at the extreme. If you live at the extreme and don't feed and water your mules, they will die. And if you can't plow to prepare the ground for planting, you starve.

The Answer to Most Things

The answer, like most things in life, is in the middle. Life is hard at the extremes. A wise person sees the extremes and searches for answers in the middle. As best I can tell, the wise live their lives in the middle. I have always been amazed by the calm when a plane flies into the eye of a hurricane. It's the most peaceful, beautiful place surrounded by the most powerful, destructive weather. It's as if the calm is fed by the chaos.

A wise person approaches life as if they were in the eye of the hurricane. For example, when someone is spinning out of control in an argument, a wise person knows that the answer is in the middle. In my work life as a leader, I was frequently charged with mediating disputes. I would hear both sides, and they would both take extreme stances. But when I finally got to the facts, they were somewhere in the middle—and the answer was in the middle too. Think about it. If you decide not to eat, you die. If you decide to eat too much, you die. When you live at the extreme, life is incredibly hard.

I once had an awesome experience while I was on a business trip to Hawaii: I got to steer a sailboat. I kept trying to steer the boat to the center point of tautness of the sail against the force of the wind. When I got it right, the boat and the wind moved in an effortless and powerful way. Just like in life, that center point was always changing, and I had to constantly adjust. That is how we have to live our lives. We must recognize reality and adjust, so we maximize the energy of life. I think of it like that plane in the eye of the hurricane. If your life is centered, then there is peace, happiness, and joy. But if the plane stands still, slows down, or goes too far into the edges, the plane will find itself being buffeted by the violence of the storm.

Wise people are constantly steering their lives to that center point where life is filled with energy rather than chaos. They are able to see things that people who live in chaos at the extreme can't see. In my opinion, that incredible place in the center where life is at its best can only be reached if you continually grow in your faith. You must always be searching for that sweet spot where your thoughts and actions are in alignment with what your Maker wants, not where the extremes of the world pull you. Like the wind and sailboat, you can't see the wind, but you can feel the wind and see the results—in life when your thoughts and actions are guided by a power you can't see but that you can feel. The results provide a calm inner spirit and an unlimited energy source. If followed, this source will guide you on a course that leads you away from the chaotic extremes and toward an abundant life.

MAXIM 25

Feed and water the mules.

Be like the sharecropper and live in the middle: Feed and water the mules. You will live a better life and make a better crop.

QUESTIONS TO PONDER:

1. Are there areas in your life where you are living at the extremes?

2. If you are, is it consuming a disproportionate amount of time and energy?

3. What can you do to return to the sweet spot in the middle where you are energetic and effective like the wind in the sail?

NEVER HAVE A BAD DAY

THERE WAS A GENTLEMAN WHO manned the security desk in the main lobby at our home office in Duluth, Georgia. His son coached football at Kent State, and he was an Atlanta Braves fan. He worked in the evenings, and I always seemed to be working late. When I would leave work, I would stop by for a few minutes and we'd talk sports. Our conversations were usually pretty brief but always uplifting. One evening, the conversation shifted from sports to life.

He told me about when he was an eighteen-year-old soldier about to ship out to Vietnam. He said his aunt had given him the greatest advice of his life. She told him to read the 23rd Psalm every day and he would never have a bad day. Then he looked me straight in the eye and said, "She was right. Every day since I was eighteen, I have read the 23rd Psalm, and I have never had a bad day."

The Lord is my shepherd, I shall not want;
He makes me lie down in green pastures.
He leads me beside still waters;
He restores my soul.
He guides me in paths of righteousness
for His name's sake.
Even though I walk through the valley of the shadow of death,
I will fear no evil;
for Thou art with me;
Thy rod and thy staff,
They comfort me.
Thou preparest a table before me
in the presence of my enemies;
Thou anointest my head with oil,
My cup overflows.
Surely goodness and mercy shall follow me
all the days of my life;
and I shall dwell in the house of the Lord forever.

That was one of those moments, a pearl of pure wisdom. From that day forward, I have made it a part of my morning routine. In reality, relatively speaking, I have never had a bad day. If he survived a tour of duty in Vietnam and never had a bad day, my life has been a blessing beyond belief. The psalm is powerful; it is impactful, and it is filled with wisdom. If there is one thing you could do to improve your life in all areas, it would be to read the 23rd Psalm every morning for the rest of your life. You will set a course to never have a bad day. You will focus on your blessings and the spiritual power available to you regardless of what life brings. Most of all you will love and be grateful for the life you have, not the one you wish you had.

MAXIM 26
Never have a bad day.

The 23rd Psalm is one of the most widely recognized verses in the Bible. It is read at funerals, displayed on walls, read by soldiers in times of war. It's been used to comfort and guide people for centuries. I am thankful to have been given the wise advice to read it every day and not to just refer to it in times of difficulty. Regardless of your beliefs, there is power and wisdom in these words. Try reading and reflecting daily on the words " . . . and surely goodness and mercy will follow you all the days of your life, and you shall dwell in the house of the Lord forever." Now that is a good day!

QUESTIONS TO PONDER:

1. Why do you think the 23rd Psalm is referred to so often in times of struggle?

2. Does it have meaning for your everyday life?

3. How will you make today a good day?

PART SIX

Maxims from
SONGS, BOOKS,
AND MOVIES

THE FIRST LINE FROM WILLIE Nelson's song, "Yesterday's Wine," talks about how miracles can happen in strange places. I think gaining wisdom is a lot like that. Life is always teaching us in everything we do, whether we know it or not. In our search for wisdom, we need to be aware that it might come at any time or in any kind of place. If we are always open-minded to learning from all of life's experiences, we won't miss wisdom when it appears.

My previous chapters contained examples of wisdom learned by listening to and learning from others, but life can teach us in many other ways. Sometimes it's words from a book that you never forget. Sometimes it's a line from a song that guides you for the rest of your life. Sometimes, it's lessons from a movie you never even intended to watch. But it's multiple lessons from different sources that bring clarity to the questions that matter. The maxims in this chapter appeared in the strangest of ways and when I least expected. My hope is they will be meaningful for you. But more than that, I hope they lead you to notice the many lessons your life is teaching you.

To a man with a hammer, every problem looks like a nail.

Anger is your enemy.

———————

To have success, study success.

———————

Live to love and love to live.

———————

If you limit what you love, you limit your life.

———————

Be your own person, not some puppet on a string.

———————

TO A MAN WITH A HAMMER, EVERY PROBLEM LOOKS LIKE A NAIL

I RECENTLY READ THREE BOOKS that helped me see the wisdom of approaching life from a broad perspective.

The first book, *Brief Answers to the Big Questions* by Stephen Hawking, was recommended by another person, and it's a book that I would never have thought to read on my own. By taking other people's recommendations, I broaden my perspective on life and think about things differently. Stephen Hawking was an unbelievable person and a renowned scientist who eventually died of ALS. He was one of those rare people who had extraordinary intelligence and became famous for his work that proved the existence of black holes in the universe.

But he could also explain complicated scientific issues in ways the non-scientific community could grasp. One of the questions Hawking attempted to answer in the book was "Is there a God?" He puts together a very scientific explanation and draws the conclusion that there is no God; that no one created the universe, and no one directs our fate. After reading his words, I struggled with how one of the smartest people who ever lived could reach the conclusion that there is no God. He could find no *scientific* evidence that God existed. For him, things that occurred in the universe ultimately had a scientific explanation. He did say that because he was a scientist, he had no other way to answer the question except from that perspective.

After reading Hawking's book, I turned to *When Breath Becomes Air* by Paul Kalanithi—a very talented neurosurgeon whose life's work regularly had him up close and personal with death as much as it did with successful surgeries. At age thirty-six, he was diagnosed with stage four cancer. When he thought like a surgeon and researcher, he questioned his faith. But when he saw life from a broad perspective as a loving father, husband, and human being, his faith grew. His life journey led him to a very powerful relationship with God, and when he died, he had love and faith at the center of his life.

I wondered how two very smart and extraordinary people could come to such very different conclusions about the most important issue in life. As I said at the beginning of this book, I believe there is a God, and it is not me or you. Doesn't it make sense that there has to be a power greater than ourselves? I am certain that if I was the know-all, be-all, I would mess this thing up so bad it couldn't be fixed.

Time after time, I have experienced a power that has guided me, comforted me, and forgiven me, and I am confident it *wasn't me*. Life at every turn has proven to be greater than me. Is life just science and that's all we have, or is there something more? In my opinion, we are spiritual beings connected to a higher power. As we become wiser, we experience moments of clarity and closeness to God. I believe in a magnificent power whose existence no scientist can prove or disprove. This power cannot be described; it can only be experienced.

The third book I read was *Poor Charlie's Almanack: The Wit and Wisdom of Charles T. Munger* edited by Peter D. Kaufman. Munger is Warren Buffett's business partner and a very wealthy individual with a deep appreciation for Benjamin Franklin. Munger has spent substantial time studying the life of the famous writer, statesman, inventor, and diplomat. Munger's worldview is multidisciplined, like Franklin's, and he believes that you must see the world from a broad perspective—and not from just one discipline such as math or physics.

The Wisdom of Munger

Munger references a famous concept when he says, "most people are trained in one model—economics, for example—and they try to solve all problems in one way. You know the old saying, 'To a man with a hammer, every problem looks like a nail.' This is a dumb way of handling problems."

I think there is a lot of wisdom in what Munger is saying. The broader your perspective, the more clearly you see reality. By focusing on one discipline, you see only a narrow slice of life. I will never know Stephen Hawking's personal journey. Nor will I know if he ultimately found any reason to believe that there is a God. I will always wonder whether he might have reached a different conclusion if he had approached the answer to the question from a broader perspective.

Most of Life's Meaning Is in a Story

When I was in college, I had a biology professor who engaged the class in a discussion of evolution versus creation. Of course, the discussion was heated and all over the place. I did not engage in the discussion, but I listened intently trying to get a read on what the professor thought. As our class time was running out, I asked the million-dollar question, "What do you believe?" His answer was a surprise, and it has stuck with me to this day. He said he believed in creation simply because it made a better story. In my continuing search for wisdom, I find that most of life's meaning is in a story that we humans interpret based on our perspectives on life.

The debate over evolution versus creation continues. New scientific facts are discovered every day that can't be ignored. Both sides have a story to tell. To me, wise people are open-minded and seek the truth. They hear the stories and then search for the meaning in their life and the lives of others. People hear a story full of wisdom and get caught up in proving or disproving the facts of the story, and they miss the wisdom in the message.

However life was created, the results appear so magnificent that they are beyond our comprehension. However it happened, we have been given life. Maybe the more important question is *why* it happened. Wise people seek to draw meaning from the message, *and* they acknowledge the proven science. This gives them a broad perspective and a deeper understanding of life that draws them closer to the truth. Be careful of narrowing your perspective as opposed to seeing life from multiple perspectives. A narrow perspective limits your wisdom and limits your life.

Munger is a successful businessman because he sees more than just the financials or the numbers. He sees the whole company and draws from his knowledge of multiple disciplines. He went to school and studied law. He made a fortune by being wise and looking beyond the numbers, beyond his legal analysis. He sees the people, the opportunities, and the challenges.

MAXIM 27

To a man with a hammer,
every problem looks like a nail.

Wise people see life from the viewpoint of multiple disciplines. They are open-minded when it comes to new ideas, and they respect the tried and true ideas that have withstood the test of time. They are constantly aware that they have a lot to learn and that most of what they thought they knew needs to be unlearned. They know that the beauty of life is the search for wisdom and truth.

Always seek wisdom and have an open mind. Always look to a greater power for guidance.

QUESTIONS TO PONDER:

1. When you look at your own life, can you see instances when you were the man with a hammer who only saw a nail?

2. Can you think of ways to broaden your perspective?

3. How would a broader perspective help you in your search for truth and wisdom?

ANGER IS YOUR ENEMY

NOT LONG AGO I CALLED one of my dear friends whose name happens to be John Lennon. John is one of the top leaders in the sales force at my former company. He's a wonderful person and someone I have always enjoyed being around. He has always treated me with respect, and I count him among the special people in my business career.

John recently lost his wife, Angela, and has continued to deal with his own health challenges. I was calling to check in and let him know I was thinking about him. We had a great conversation, and John—as he always did—put his best foot forward in the face of the adversity he was facing. Also, like he typically does, he turned the conversation to me. He said, "Chess you always had the ability to keep your senses and bring calm when everybody else was in a panic. You were good at not getting caught up in the emotions of the moment. While we were stressing out, you were calm."

John and I experienced a lot of change in our time working

together, including multiple leadership, compensation, and product changes. These transitions always had a huge impact on John's business, both positive and negative. When he had concerns about the new developments, he would give me a call or come see me. He knew I would tell him what I thought and not overreact to anything he said or to the uncertainty of the change. John, who is a passionate man, also knew he could say what he was feeling. It didn't matter if he was fired up about the change or if he was upset about it, we would share ideas on how the change could help his business. Working together, we were both better prepared to maximize the results of the change.

My experience in business and in life is that wise people always keep things in perspective. Remember, things are never as bad as they seem—or as good as they seem. Like the changes John and I discussed, the impact was never as good or as bad as we first thought. It's all about how you react to the change. John and I understood that the change was happening, and it was okay to say what we thought, but once we accepted that it was happening, we had to accept it and not let our emotions make us upset. The more we focused on what we didn't like, the longer it was going to take before we were able to take advantage of it. I have discussions today with people who are still angry about something that happened ten years ago, while others embraced the changes and grew their business to a level that they never thought possible.

A wise person will guard against overreacting with their words and their actions. And people who are *looking* for wisdom need to do the same: react and take action, but don't overreact.

When you keep your composure instead of becoming angry and upset, your clarity to deal with things improves.

Several years ago, I read a book called *Days of Grace* by the great tennis player Arthur Ashe. He grew up playing tennis in the segregated South and had a coach who gave him great advice when he was just a young kid. He taught Arthur to stay focused on the match and not be distracted by the prejudice of the crowd or the line judge. If he lost his cool, it would affect his performance and limit his opportunities in the future.

There is a saying in sports psychology that anger is what happens to you right before the sports gods destroy you. It is possible for players to get angry and improve their short-term performance. But what's more likely to happen is that they will come unglued from their anger, and their performance will tank. For athletes to reach their peak performance, they must be in the zone where focus and positive energy drive their performance. I have expanded this concept to apply to all areas of life. Anger is what happens just before the sports gods, the work gods, and the family gods destroy you. My life experience has taught me that anger is not the answer. My first memory of life teaching me what anger could do was as a kid playing backyard football.

I hated to lose a backyard football game. If someone on my team wasn't giving his best and we were losing, I would get so angry that I would yell, scream, push, shove, punch—whatever I could do to win. I can only remember losing one game. In that game, I got so mad at a cousin that after that game, our friendship was never the same. It was the first time I was cognizant that anger was my enemy, and that it could destroy a friendship.

I cannot think of one time when anger was the best response. Anger gets you kicked out of athletic competitions, damages relationships, and makes enemies unnecessarily.

Wise People Stay in the Zone

As our life unfolds and crap happens, a wise person, just like an athlete, works to stay in the zone. When an athlete is in the zone, everything slows down. If you are a running back in football, you see the field with ultra-clarity. You run to daylight, your football senses are at the maximum, and you perform at your highest athletic ability.

I think the same is true in life. If you can stay centered and not let your emotions cause you to lose control but, instead, react appropriately, then life gets better. As you know, for me, this is a lifelong struggle, because my nature is to get angry when things are not going my way. So over the years, life has constantly needed to teach me this lesson. I have come a long way from that kid playing backyard football. Today, I am closer to *Cool Hand Luke* most of the time, thanks to the guidance of a simple maxim: Anger is your enemy.

Wise People Are Aware of Their Emotions

A wise person should always be aware of their emotions and strive to stay centered or in the zone. That's where you make your best decisions. My experience is that if your decisions are filled with anger, fear, or animosity, you typically don't make the wisest choice available. You waste your energy on all of those negative emotions instead of focusing your energy on what needs to be done.

Our lives and the lives of those around us are made up of the decisions we make and how we treat people. It is one of the hardest things to do to keep your emotions from taking control, especially in the case of instant anger. Usually something happens, and you lash out verbally or, in the worst cases, physically. The results are never good. At work—just like those days playing backyard football—my biggest challenge was when someone was about to do something that I believed was going to get us beat or hurt the company. My first reaction was to get angry, which would lead to an argument. The argument would lead to both sides just digging in on their position. All it did was waste a lot of energy and make getting to the right decision more difficult. When I took a deep breath and kept our focus on finding a solution, I ultimately got better results.

MAXIM 28
Anger is your enemy.

It was good to hear John's words about me staying calm in the face of chaos. We need a constant reminder about the wisdom of keeping our focus instead of getting caught up in the emotions of the moment and making a snap decision that we will regret. Remember, anger is what happens to you right before the _____ (you fill in the blank) gods destroy you. A wise person is aware of what emotions are influencing their decisions and actions. The wisest people react appropriately.

QUESTIONS TO PONDER:

1. Think about a time when your emotions made you lose control of a situation.

2. Did losing control make things better or worse?

3. In what way?

4. Do you have a plan for handling a similar situation if it arises again?

TO HAVE SUCCESS,
STUDY SUCCESS

FROM THE TIME I WAS a kid up until today, I have always been interested in how someone can be the very best at what they do. I have a passion for what separates those who are the best at what they do from others in their profession. Most of the people I have studied were sports figures—superstar athletes and coaches like Vince Lombardi, Michael Jordan, Nick Saban, and Pat Summitt to name a few. It all started with Ted Williams back when I was a boy, and I read that when he was a kid, he wanted to be the greatest hitter who ever lived.

As a young baseball player, I thought that would be the ultimate achievement in sports. But unfortunately, I never hit like Ted! The best I could do was become a .300 high school hitter—not quite what it takes to be in the Hall of Fame. As an adult, I read multiple books on his life. My conclusion is if you want to improve as a hitter, Ted is your man to study. He had an amazing understanding of the science of hitting. Ted, in my opinion was the greatest hitter who ever lived. Reading and learning about Ted's life led me to ask the question: If you want success, should you study success?

Over my sixty-three years of life, I have come to believe the maxim, "If you want success, study success." I always wanted to be a good coach: It didn't matter if I was coaching a high school baseball player in the summer, coaching my kids' teams in youth sports, or coaching my team at work. I have spent hundreds of hours studying great coaches, and I have taken their coaching lessons and applied them in other areas of my life. My library contains books on a wide range of successful people. I studied them not to become them, but to learn from them. Doing this has had a positive influence on my life and helped me grow a little wiser. Anytime I spent looking at why people were *unsuccessful* never yielded the results I got from studying success. Early in my business career, I was asked to study individuals who were not successful at certain aspects of our business such as getting an insurance license or making a sale. While I might have found some interesting information, I never found the keys to success. It never made sense to me to spend valuable time studying people who were doing it wrong rather than people who were doing it right.

Of all the sports people I studied, the wisest and most successful by my standards was John Wooden. Coach Wooden won ten national championships in college basketball over a twelve-year period and was named by ESPN as the number one coach of all time. But he didn't just play at the top of his profession—he succeeded in all areas of his life. I would highly recommend you read everything you can find on Coach Wooden.

One of the most amazing speeches I ever heard was by ninety-two-year-old Wooden. The evening started at a pre-event where folks had the opportunity to have their picture taken with and get an autograph from the coach. I ran into a former business associate there—Deward Dopson. Prior to a successful business career, "Dop" had been a successful basketball coach. He was probably in his seventies by this time, and he was as excited as a kid at Christmas. He was about to meet his hero and have him sign an old worn-out book that was highlighted on every page.

The book was written by Coach Wooden and had inspired and guided Dop as a young coach and later in business. It hit me then what a powerful impact Coach Wooden had made on one of the finest men I knew. In that moment, I realized that I was in the presence of a man who had made a positive influence on millions of people, including myself. When it was time for Wooden's speech, he was aided to a stool at the side of the stage, where he sat, without any notes at ninety-two years old, and he talked for over a hour. He taught the fifteen blocks of his Pyramid of Success. He talked about things like cooperation, self-control, team spirit, and other principles that led to his success; not just in sports but also in life. It was by far the most meaningful talk I have ever heard. He led a life full of wisdom. Coach Wooden's life reflected everything that makes a great coach and a great man.

One day, as I reflected on all the people I had read about and studied both in sports and outside of sports, from preachers, politicians, generals, war heroes—from business leaders to Mother Teresa, I began to wonder if I had become a mile wide and an inch deep in my efforts. What could I learn if I narrowed my focus down to just the people that I admired the most? After some thought, I decided that the greatest person who ever lived was Jesus of Nazareth. So, in 2017, I decided to spend my morning comparing John Wooden and Jesus of Nazareth. What did they have that separated them from the others I admired?

When I studied the life of Jesus, I found no one ever walked the face of the earth who lived a better life. His life and teachings are the wisest I have studied, and He continues to change the world to this day. Over two thousand years after He lived, people continue to describe Him as the Prince of Peace, the Good Shepherd, and the Son of God. His life was a walk of faith, and many of the people I mention in this chapter have been guided by His teachings. He taught the power of faith in God. I would encourage everyone to study His life, His teachings, and to consider the power of faith in God. Faith is the only path I have found that leads to a truly abundant life. My point here is that there is wisdom in studying His life, and you can decide whether He was the greatest person who ever lived. It doesn't matter if you believe Jesus was a human being or the Messiah: I contend that there is no better example of how to live life.

Once I began to compare what I knew about Jesus with what I knew about Coach Wooden, it quickly became clear that Coach Wooden was hands down better than most of us. His edge was his faith; his life was guided by the life of Jesus. Now I am no Biblical scholar, but as best I can tell, Jesus' faith in God separated Him from anyone who has ever lived. If we seek wisdom, and if it leads to a spiritual journey, it will eventually lead to the importance of faith in God.

I would encourage all of you who want to be good coaches or good people to study the lives of these two men. Their teaching and their actions were guided by their faith. Their extraordinary lives were anchored by their faith. What is life without faith? Is it possible to have a life of true meaning without faith in God?

When I reflect on faith, it has been my fuel in life. It's been my access to a power greater than myself. It has helped me experience the good things in life at a deeper level. The birth of my first grandchild and the journey into retirement are recent events that have been incredible because of this unseen power. Faith has given me comfort when going through life's struggles: the death of my dad, the ups and downs of fatherhood, the challenges at work. The lives of the successful people I have known and those I have studied and respected were grounded in faith. Their faith made them better leaders, coaches, mothers, fathers, and just better people with more meaningful lives. Faith in God is the source of all things unseen: spiritual energy, love, hope, courage, and peace.

The wiser we become, the more faith we will have in God and the more these unseen, limitless powers will transform our lives. You can't explain it; you can only live it. And the fruits you harvest will be in the form of a more abundant life.

MAXIM 29

To have success, study success.

The wise spend time learning from others. Not to be them but to learn from them. The more I meet and study people I admire, the clearer it becomes that faith has been a powerful part of their success. As I reflect on my life, I am in awe at the power of faith and perplexed by how much of this power I have left untapped. But I am confident in its transformational effect on our lives.

QUESTIONS TO PONDER:

1. Who do you consider to be the greatest person who has ever lived?

2. Why do you think that was, and how do you define greatness?

3. What qualities separated that person from the rest?

LIVE TO LOVE AND LOVE TO LIVE

SEVERAL MONTHS AGO, I WENT to bed and fell asleep with the TV on. I woke up in the middle of the night, and the movie *Country Strong* was on. Usually when this happens, I turn the TV off and go back to sleep. But for whatever reason, I was drawn into this movie. Two ideas expressed in the movie stuck with me, and I continue to think about the wisdom of them. I am paraphrasing here:

Love a lot of things—that is what matters in life.
Love and fame don't live in the same house.

I want to concentrate on the first sentence because it is the one that rings truest to me based upon my beliefs. (The second is great food for thought, and could be something to consider if you are dealing with fame. I have never had that problem.) Love God, love people, love yourself, and love life. Love is the most magnificently powerful force in existence. For me, my life has gotten better when I was focused on love rather than on my other emotions. In life, there are a lot of ways to use your emotional energy. You can hate, you can judge, you can fear, you can complain, you can worry, or you can love.

I can't think of a time when my life improved because I felt those negative emotions. As I reflect on my life, the happiest most rewarding moments are those that are filled with love. It's taking a walk on the beach with Trisha. It's holding my sons for the first time. It's Thanksgiving with the family. It's seeing our grandson smile. It's all the moments grounded in love. The more we live to love and love to live, the more meaningful and fulfilling our lives become.

What It Means to Live to Love and Love to Live

1. Love God with all your heart and soul.

It's a tall order, but it will yield powerful results as you journey down life's path. The wiser I become, the more I love God. When my life spins out of control and thing become chaotic, the only way I have found to weather these storms is to look up and focus my thoughts and actions on loving God.

It's like steering that sailboat I talked about earlier. Most of the time, I didn't have the boat pointed in the optimum direction, but the closer I came the better the boat performed. Like the boat, I never have my love for God where it needs to be. The closer I come to loving God with all my heart and soul, the better life becomes.

2. Love people.

That means family, friends, enemies, and all others. Love them for who they are—not who you wish they were. Have you ever paid attention to how much of our time is spent judging others versus loving others? Have you met someone for the first time and—based on their looks—decided you didn't want to get to know them? Remember the guy I met in Texas who asked if I would buy him lunch? Because I looked past his appearance and acted with kindness, both our lives were blessed.

3. Love yourself.

The great basketball coach, John Wooden, quotes his father as saying, "Son, don't ever think you are better than somebody else, but never forget you're just as good as anybody." Always treat yourself and others that way. Just keep in mind that most people who try to make you feel less than you are just want to prove they are superior to you—but they are not.

In the short run, it's easy to play down to who and what others want you to be. The wise people I know do not obsess about what others think. They look in the mirror and understand that they need to live a life that makes them proud of the person in the mirror. Even more important, they want their God to be pleased with who

continued

they have become and how they live. You are worthy
of love.

4. Love life.

Life is short, and it is precious. Love it. Spend your time
focused on loving life. Be grateful for the blessings of life.
See the warmth of the sunshine, not the heat of the day.
See the blessing of rain, not the lack of sunshine. Be thank-
ful you're alive. Count your blessings, not your problems.
Love the blessing that is life.

Loving Others Versus Judging Others

Have you ever noticed how much time we spend criticizing and
judging those we love most? We spend our time focused on *what*
we want them to change; not seeing *who* they are. Our thoughts
and action are driven by what we want, without considering
what's happening in their lives. As we grow wiser, we become
aware of this behavior. This issue continues to be a big challenge in my life. It's human nature, but judging others is not in
alignment with the four points we've discussed. As best I can
tell, we are called to love others, not to judge them.

We should all become aware of our thoughts about people, our first impressions, our desire for them to be like us, our
thoughts about our superiority to others. We seem to be a better
judge of what others need to change versus what we need to
change. We should also become more aware of how often we
criticize others instead of loving them. Are our words based on

our dislike of others or our love for others? Nothing makes a relationship more challenging than criticism. It doesn't matter what the relationship is: It can be a marriage, a friendship, a business relationship. The wiser we become, the more we strive to understand the importance of accepting and respecting people for who they are.

We have the ability to make people feel special and appreciated. We also have the ability to make people run and hide when they see us coming. It has been my experience that it all comes down to the obvious: treat others like you want to be treated. Put yourself in the shoes of the other person. Given their particular circumstances, would you want to be judged and criticized or would you be helped more by being heard and understood?

My work career was always about building relationships. Early in my career, when I worked to resolve issues with members of our sales force, I would start with *my* opinion and what *I* thought needed to change. This behavior inevitably led to an argument and the realization that I had no understanding of what the real issues were from their point of view. It didn't take long for me to realize that most leaders didn't care what I thought until I better understood their concerns and challenges. I think this is true in all relationships.

As we become more aware of our own thoughts and actions, we change how we relate to people. When they feel that you love and respect them, they become more open to your words and your guidance. One of life's realities is we cannot change others; they must change themselves. My life experiences are teaching me that the more we accept and love people rather than criticize and hurt them, the more impactful and influential our life will be on others' lives. Wise people treat others like they would want to be treated.

MAXIM 30
Live to love and love to live.

I believe God is love and our highest calling is to love God, love others, love ourselves, and love life. As we become wiser, we grow in our understanding of the power of love. The more we live a life guided by love, the more we are going to love to live.

QUESTIONS TO PONDER:

1. How are you using or not using love to your best advantage in your search for wisdom?

2. When you reflect on your life, what are your happiest moments?

3. Did love play a role?

4. Do you spend more time judging others or loving others?

5. Do you strive to treat others like you want to be treated?

IF YOU LIMIT WHAT YOU LOVE, YOU LIMIT YOUR LIFE

IF YOU LIMIT WHAT YOU love, you limit your life. I had never really thought about this until one morning when I was reflecting on the message from *Country Strong*: Love a lot of things; that is what matters in life. I began thinking about things I thought I didn't like and how once I tried them how much I loved them. I never had any interest in going to a University of Georgia women's gymnastics meet. When I finally went to one, I loved it. The competition and athleticism was like nothing I had ever seen. Trisha and I are now season ticket holders. There's no telling how many great experiences I have missed in my sixty-three years by assuming I did not like something. Be careful when you say no to something new. By doing so, you may miss the experience of a lifetime.

A case in point: I was in Colorado on a company trip, and several people were going zip-lining. They had just opened the zip line that day, and we were some of the first to do the course.

I had no desire to zip-line, but thank God, my wife, Trisha, wanted to do it. It was truly a memorable experience. According to the guide, it was one of the most extreme zip lines in the world, and our adventure was filled with high winds and rain. There were five zip lines from 250 feet to 1800 feet long at heights of 550 feet. We had to cross two suspended rope bridges, and the only way off the mountain when you were finished zip-lining was to rappel 180 feet down the mountain.

The course was incredible. The view was amazing. The feeling of knowing the zip line was the only thing protecting us from a free fall into the bottom of canyon was an extreme adrenaline rush. After our third zip, we had to walk across 200 feet of suspended rope bridges. From that vantage point, we could see the final two zips—they made the first three pale in comparison. Before stepping out onto the bridge, we were informed this was the point of no return. Once you set foot on the bridge, the only way down was to finish the course. But as we were crossing the bridge, the weather changed suddenly. Strong wind and light rain set in. That's when the guides got concerned.

Before letting us do the next zip, they radioed down to base camp. Even though the winds were gusting at twenty-two miles per hour, the safest thing was to complete the course. It was windy, raining, and getting colder by the minute, and the guides were moving things along in the safest, fastest manner possible. Trisha went first, and I could see her reach the platform. I was ready to go next when the guides stopped me. I began to get concerned that something had happened to Trisha. We had no radio contact with the other platform for approximately ten minutes before they finally gave me the go. When I got to the other side, I discovered Trisha was mostly okay. She was too short to reach the platform, and they had needed to use a rope ladder to unhook her. On the final zip, only one person reached the platform. The headwinds were so strong that we stopped 100 feet out. We had to grab the zip line and pull ourselves in!

It was an incredible adventure for a guy who is not a thrill-seeker, and it was something that I simply wouldn't have done normally. Now it's a memory for a lifetime.

Be Wise About Saying No to Things

If we have never actually participated in a certain activity, it's probably not very wise to say we don't like it. It's easy to sit around and say we don't like this or that, but what good is doing that when we've never actually tried that particular thing? This is coming from a guy who is the biggest creature of habit ever. I worked for the same company for over thirty-six years. I have attended the same church for fifty-seven years. But every new place I've been and every new experience I've had have made my life more rewarding. It didn't matter if I traveled to a small town in South Georgia to watch a high school baseball game or to Spain on business—they all counted as adventures, and I am thankful I went.

There is wisdom in keeping your mind open to new things that will improve your life. The key is you. Before you say you don't like something, ask yourself:

· Have I ever done this before? If the answer is no, be careful before you say you don't like it.

· How can you not like something you have never done?

· Will it make my life better or the lives of others better?

MAXIM 31

If you limit what you love, you limit your life.

Remember when you limit what you love, you limit your life. Don't be afraid to love new things and places.

QUESTIONS TO PONDER:

1. What is something you think you don't like (or are afraid of) that could possibly become today's new thing you love or tomorrow's new adventure?

2. Can you be brave enough to create a new bucket list?

BE YOUR OWN PERSON,
NOT SOME PUPPET ON A STRING

WHEN I WAS A KID, radio station WPLO was Atlanta's premier country music station. Although my dad didn't listen to a lot of radio, when he did, it was WPLO. It was a big treat if we were going somewhere and he turned on the car radio because I always loved to listen to music. I remember a song called "You've Got to Stand for Something" that was popular at the time. It talked about being your own man and not acting like a puppet on a string. For some reason that stuck with me. Growing up and as an adult, whenever I was faced with either following the crowd or being "my own man," I would think of that song.

As you read this book, remember, it is your life: You've got to figure it out. My answer or my way of looking at things might not be important to you, and that's okay. What's important is that you choose based on what you believe to be true, not what I believe. I don't think it's necessary that you change any of your beliefs. But I do think we should always examine what we believe based on what we have learned. Beware of blindly following the crowd. Don't believe something just because it's what others believe. Don't do what others do just to fit in. Your action should align with your beliefs, and your beliefs should be forged in wisdom from within and from above.

Why Your Uniqueness Is Important

We are all unique individuals. We all have our own talents that make us special to this world. There is no other individual like you and no other who can do what you can do. A wise person understands that their uniqueness is what gives value to their existence. As we seek to grow in wisdom, we must search for who we really are. That search can start with you asking the question, "Who am I?" Don't confuse who you are with what you have done.

You are not somebody's wife or someone's husband. You are more than what you do or who you are related to. You are a unique individual who is like no other. An amazing spirit lives in you. Your challenge is to always be moving in the direction that your heart and spirit are leading you. Look up for answers. Seek guidance from above. Pray for wisdom. Anytime I have been my own man, it has paid dividends—for my character, my self-esteem, and, ultimately, in the respect of others. When I followed the crowd, knowing my actions were not aligned with my beliefs, it led me to regret, and I learned it's better to be respected than it is to be liked for the wrong reasons.

This doesn't mean that you should be a contrarian. It means to be wise and know when it is important to be the voice of reason. For individuals who have played sports, you know you don't always agree with the play the coach calls, but it's the coach's call. You run the play to the best of your ability. That's true with most things in life. But if it is immoral, illegal, or just plain stupid, you might need to recommend an audible. If you want to be respected and have your judgment valued when it matters, be your own person.

Know Your Role

There will be times when your team is searching for the right answer or the best decision. A wise leader will express what he or she believes, but will remain open to the facts and the possibility that there could be a better answer out there. A leader will call the play. Sometimes he or she will be right. But sometimes it will be obvious that your recommendation would have been a better call. Use these situations to grow wiser and become a better leader and decision maker, because at some point, you could be the ultimate decision maker, and you will want to be guided by wisdom and experience.

When you are the head coach or the ultimate decision maker, be wise and listen to those whose opinions you trust. But remember, the final decision is yours. You want to win or lose based on your game plan. Nothing is worse than for a head coach to lose because he or she ran someone else's play. Instead, be your own person and follow your heart. Look up for guidance. The good Lord will always lead you in the right direction. It won't necessarily be the easiest path, but your heart will not mislead you even when your head might.

MAXIM 32

Be your own person,
not some puppet on a string.

Spend time understanding who you are and what you believe. As you grow in wisdom, your true beliefs will become clearer. Know that the world needs you, not an imitation of who others want you to be. When the crowd is heading in the wrong direction, look for opportunities to lead them in the right direction.

QUESTIONS TO PONDER:

1. Think about a time when you followed the crowd and things turned out badly.

2. Think about another time when you decided not to follow the crowd and you were saved from a bad situation.

3. What did you learn from both situations?

4. Did you learn more about who you are and what it means to be your own person?

EPILOGUE

IN SHARING THE LESSONS THAT I have learned in my search for wisdom, my intent is not to tell you how to live your life or what to believe. I have shared them in the hopes that they will give you some insight and motivation to—

See the value of centering your life in a lifelong search for wisdom. As you become wiser, all areas of your life will get better.

Realize that wisdom is available to all who seek it, no matter who you are or what you have or have not done. Wisdom is a bottomless well that is available to you in whatever quantities you choose to consume.

Understand that the search for wisdom is a lifelong journey. I assume that most folks are like me—and we are only a short distance down the road.

Discover that the search for wisdom is an exciting and rewarding journey.

Understand that God communicates to us through our life experiences. The secret is to be wise enough to listen, change, and grow.

Realize that we become wiser by listening, observing, and learning from the wisdom of others who have learned the lesson life is trying to teach.

Always look up for answers to life's challenges and blessings and to seek guidance in all areas of your life from your Creator.

They say the best time to plant a tree was twenty-five years ago. The second-best time is right now. The same is true for our search for wisdom. If you are led to begin your journey or to continue the journey, it might be a good idea to do what Solomon did and pray for wisdom—and seek, observe, and learn what life teaches you. The beauty of life is that every journey is different. There is no how-to guide to wisdom. There are only the unique life experiences you'll find on your path. If you desire to have life and have it abundantly, begin your search and follow it where it leads.

Go Out and Take Advantage of It

I will end with one more story—about one of my heroes in life, Erk Russell, who was the defensive coordinator for the University of Georgia football team in 1980 when they won the national championship. Out of all the coaches I have read about and studied, to me, he was the master motivator. Georgia had, in my opinion, the greatest college football player of my lifetime: Herschel Walker. Russell's words of wisdom to Walker on the day of the national championship game were, "It's a great day the Lord has given us. Let's go out and take advantage of it."

No matter where you are in your life's journey, no matter what your circumstances, good or bad, today is not just a great day; it's a glorious day the Lord has given us. Let's go out and take advantage of it. For today, like no other, can be filled with more wisdom, love, and understanding than any other day in your life. Live it to its fullest.

May God bless your journey.

"Happy is the man who finds wisdom,
And the man who gets understanding,
For the gain from it is better than gain
From silver, and its profit better than gold.
She is more precious than jewels,
And nothing you desire can compare with her."

Proverbs 3:13–15

ABOUT THE AUTHOR

I GREW UP IN A small town in rural Georgia. I was raised by grounded and humble parents who were not perfect but who always loved us and made us feel special. I never felt as if I were blessed with exceptional abilities, but I always found a way to make the most of my God-given talents. I grew up playing team sports and loved being a positive influence on my teammates. I believe my gift or my "edge" has been my ability to influence those around me to use their talents to become better versions of themselves.

I have always loved coaching people. I am blessed to have been surrounded by wise people who shared their life's wisdom with me. Thank goodness I learned and absorbed many of those valuable lessons and have been able to share those lessons with others. Now at age sixty-three, my goal is to plant the seeds of wisdom to help more people reach their potential.

I am a 1978 graduate of the University of Georgia, and I worked in various leadership roles for Primerica, the largest financial services marketing organization in North America, for more than thirty-six years. I served as the company's chief marketing officer from 2010 to June 2018, and I was pleased that my advice and wisdom were sought throughout my career by CEOs, executives, highly successful members of our sales force, the management team, employees, and our representatives.

I've spent a lifetime studying successful people from all walks of life. I believe my observations, which have proven to be invaluable in my own journey, will help my readers become better versions of who they were meant to be, no matter what career or life path they are on.